"If your parents were divorced, you need to read this compelling book. *Breaking the Cycle of Divorce* acts like an inoculation against the divorce epidemic, preventing its spread from generation to generation. It will assure you that your marriage *can* be for a lifetime and give you a very practical road map to get you there."

SHAUNTI FELDHAHN, author of *For Women Only*

"Dr. John Trent is honest. He is vulnerable, and he is right! Adult children of divorce (like me) *can* begin a new cycle of successful marriage in their family. I know because I've been married 41 years! Start reading, because this book gives you practical steps to take you to a lifelong love."

LINDA DILLOW, author of *Calm My Anxious Heart*
and co-author of *Intimate Issues*

"While acknowledging the detrimental influence of parental divorce on children, this book gives compelling evidence that the negative power of parental example can be broken. John Trent is 'living proof' that the insights of this book can lead to a successful marriage."

GARY D. CHAPMAN, PH.D., author of *The Five Love Languages* and *The Four Seasons of Marriage*

"John Trent takes the family portrait of divorce and changes the frame to one of hope. He shows us how to paint over the broken lines of divorce with brushstrokes of enduring love, gives us the tools to break the cycle, and shares how to create a legacy of love for a lifetime."

SHARON JAYNES, author of *Becoming the Woman of His Dreams* and *Becoming a Woman Who Listens to God*

San Diego Christian College
2100 Greenfield Drive
El Cajon, CA 92019

FOCUS ON THE FAMILY
R E S O U R C E S

BREAKING
THE CYCLE OF
DIVORCE

JOHN TRENT, Ph.D.
with Larry K. Weeden

Tyndale House Publishers, Inc.
Carol Stream, Illinois

A Focus on the Family book published by
Tyndale House Publishers, Carol Stream, Illinois 60188

TYNDALE is a registered trademark of Tyndale House Publishers, Inc.
Tyndale's quill logo is a trademark of Tyndale House Publishers, Inc.

All Scripture quotations, unless otherwise indicated, are taken from the *Holy Bible,
New International Version®*. NIV®. Copyright © 1973, 1978, 1984 by International
Bible Society. Used by permission of Zondervan Publishing House. All rights
reserved. Scripture quotations marked (NASB) are taken from the *New American Standard Bible®*. Copyright The Lockman Foundation 1960, 1962, 1963, 1968, 1971,
1972, 1973, 1975, 1977, 1995. Used by permission.

People's names and certain details of their stories have been changed to protect the
privacy of the individuals involved.

Editors: Mick Silva, Kathy Davis
Cover design by: Joseph Sapulich
Cover photograph © by MedioImages/Getty Images. All rights reserved.

Published in association with the literary agency of Alive Communications, Inc.,
7680 Goddard Street, Suite 200, Colorado Springs, CO 80920,
www.alivecommunications.com

Library of Congress Cataloging-in-Publication Data
Trent, John T.
  Breaking the cycle of divorce : how your marriage can succeed even if your
parents' didn't / by John Trent, with Larry Weeden.
     p. cm.
  "A Focus on the Family book."
  ISBN-13: 978-1-58997-004-5
  ISBN-10: 1-58997-004-7
  1. Divorce—Religious aspects—Christianity. 2. Marriage—Religious aspects—
Christianity. I. Weeden, Larry K. II. Title.
  BT707.T74 2006
  646.7'8—dc22

                                                    2005034854

Printed in the United States of America
1 2 3 4 5 6 7 8 9 / 12 11 10 09 08 07 06

*In loving memory of Zoa L. Trent, beloved mother
and a world-class example of someone who used God's love
to "reverse the curse" for her children and many others*

෨

Contents

Acknowledgments

My thanks go to Cecil Price, professional researcher par excellence, for his help in finding statistics and other material used in this book.

I'd also like to thank my friend Jim McGuire, who served as a technical go-between when my e-mail and that of my co-writer didn't want to get along with each other. I'm glad Jim was up some late nights to get chapter attachments from one of us to the other.

As always, my agent, Lee Hough at Alive Communications, was a great help in pulling together the pieces of the project and looking out for my best interests.

On the personal side, my wife, Cindy, and our daughters, Kari and Laura, deserve praise for their loving support and encouragement. I couldn't do the work I do if I didn't have them all solidly in my corner. They're my biggest fans, and that means more to me than I can say.

My brothers, Jeff and Joe, are likewise a source of great encouragement as I work on writing projects. In this book, they're also a part of the cast of characters.

Finally, my thanks go to the Focus on the Family team of professionals who have worked so hard to help shape, package, and present this book in an outstanding way.

THE
CHALLENGE

*Children of divorce have no idea how
to create and maintain a healthy relationship
themselves. Typically, therefore, the idea
of getting married fills them with both
joy and dread at the same time.*

I magine growing up in a big city in the eastern United States, having never set foot outside the "concrete jungle." One day a person you care for a great deal asks you to paint a picture of the Arizona desert in spring bloom, with flowering cacti of various kinds and a brightly colored carpet of wildflowers covering the sand—a scene you've never witnessed or even viewed in photographs.

Would you be able to do it?

Almost certainly you'd find it impossible, even if you had artistic talent. How could you hope to paint a landscape you had never seen? You might worry about hurting your loved one's feelings; you might wish desperately that you could satisfy the request. But you'd find yourself asking, "What does one kind of cactus look like, let alone a dozen different kinds? And since when do cacti bloom? And while we're at it, what's a wildflower?"

Adult children of divorce who are considering the possibility of marriage—or who are already married and struggling to keep it together—face a challenge that seems nearly as inconceivable. Like every human being, they want to be loved and accepted. Like most people, they long to find those things in a marriage relationship that will be strong and thriving and mutually fulfilling "for as long as we both shall live."

Unfortunately, those adult children of divorce have never seen such a marriage relationship. They have no idea what it looks like. Their only experience is with a relationship that, for any of a thousand reasons, didn't last. In their experience, when the going gets tough, men and women bail out of a "bad" marriage.

A number of surveys and studies have discovered that adult children of divorce are far more likely to get divorced themselves than are the adult children of intact families (i.e., families in which Mom and Dad did not divorce).

So these children of divorce very often have no idea how to create and maintain a healthy relationship themselves. Typically, therefore, the idea of getting married fills them with both joy and dread at the same time. As Judith Wallerstein, one of the leading researchers on the effects of divorce, puts it, "When children of divorce become adults, they are badly frightened that their relationships will fail, just like the most important relationship in their parents' lives failed. They mature with a keen sense that their growing-up experiences did not prepare them for love, commitment, trust, marriage, or even for the nitty-gritty of handling and resolving conflicts. . . . [T]hey are haunted by powerful ghosts from their childhoods that tell them that they, like their parents, will not succeed."[1]

Those fears are well founded. A number of surveys and studies have discovered that adult children of divorce are far more likely to get divorced themselves than are the adult children of intact families (i.e., families in which Mom and Dad did not divorce).[2] Depending on the survey, the child of divorce is at least two to four times more likely to divorce.

As if the divorce statistics weren't scary enough, the children of divorce are also more prone to other problems. For instance, they are twice as likely as children from intact homes to drop out of high school. They're twice as likely to become teen parents and unmarried parents. They're also far more likely to become dependent on welfare as adults.[3]

THERE IS HOPE

If you're reading this as an adult child of divorce, you're probably familiar with those statistics and the fear they produce.

You may be wondering, as I suggested at the beginning, how you can possibly be expected to paint a picture of something you've never seen—how you can have a strong, intact marriage when your own parents' marriage failed. And you're probably wondering whether this book can really help.

To you, the anxious reader, I have two things to say here at the outset. *First and foremost, yes, it is possible to break the cycle of divorce.* You *can* learn to create and maintain a healthy, strong, lasting marriage relationship. You *can* learn to paint that picture of something you haven't yet seen. There is real hope for your future and your marriage.

Second, it may encourage you to know that I don't address this topic as an academic who simply thought it would make for an interesting study. No, this book is rooted in my own experience and grows out of my own passion and need to know. You see, I, too, am an adult child of divorce. My father actually went through three divorces, my mother through two.

So, like you, as I met and fell in love with the person of my dreams, I had to wonder whether I could enjoy a healthy marriage. When conflicts arose after the wedding, I had to consider whether we could work through our differences.

Could I succeed where my parents had failed, or was I doomed to repeat their mistakes, their choices, . . . their patterns?

Because I was privileged to marry the most wonderful woman in the world, because of lessons I've learned along the way (from my mom and others), and especially because of God's grace, I will have been married for 27 years by the time this book releases, and the future looks even brighter than the past. My wife, Cindy, and I are living proof that the cycle of divorce can be broken. My parents' marital failure does *not* have to dictate the fate of our relationship, and your parents' divorce doesn't have to doom your marriage either.

You, an adult child of divorce, can create a strong, lasting marriage. When conflicts arise between you and your spouse, the two of you can work through them and find healthy resolution. In the face of other challenges (health issues, the everyday trials of life, etc.), you and your mate can draw closer together rather than drifting apart.

Walk with me through the pages of this book and let me show you how to start a new cycle in your family. It all begins, as we'll see in chapter 1, with recognizing that because you grew up in a home of divorce, you also grew up facing a greater challenge than you may have imagined. For, realize it or not, even in the twenty-first century, you're facing the effects of a curse.

QUESTIONS FOR REFLECTION AND APPLICATION

1. As a child of divorce, what is your greatest fear in getting or being married yourself?

2. What do you think a healthy marriage should look like? Why?

3. Right now, on a scale from 1 (no confidence at all) to 10 (absolutely certain), how confident are you that you can break the cycle of divorce and build a strong and lasting marriage?

chapter One

UNDER THE CURSE

The picture is clear that children and adults whose parents divorce really are living under a curse. And the curse spreads from generation to generation until someone manages to break it and establish new patterns.

I n the introduction, I had you imagine being asked to paint a landscape that you'd never seen. Now let me give you another word picture to help you understand what adult children of divorce (ACODs) are up against.

Today, when we hear the word *curse*, we envision a horror movie or an image out of a Stephen King–type novel of someone standing in a graveyard at midnight, shaking a bloody chicken leg at us. Those are imaginary pictures that may haunt us but don't really touch us. But the "curse" you and I grew up with, if you're from a divorced family, is real.

In the Bible, when it speaks of someone's being "under a curse," the image is that of a stream that has been dammed up. Much of the Holy Land is arid. So streams flowing with fresh, life-giving water—when they can be found—are vitally important.

Imagine, then, that you're stumbling through a desert, exhausted and thirsty. Your water gave out days ago, and your mouth feels as dry as the sand. The relentless sun bakes your brain and blinds your eyes. The bleached-white bones of a long-dead camel remind you of how perilous your own situation is.

What keeps you going? What gives you hope? You know that somewhere up ahead—not too far now—is a spring-fed stream. Even in the driest times, this stream is known to keep flowing. If you can just get to it, this water will give you new strength and energy, refreshing you enough to complete your return to civilization.

At last, the stream comes into view as you crest a hill! At first you're afraid it might be a mirage. But as you lurch down the far side of the hill, gathering speed as you go and drawing closer and closer, you recognize that it is, indeed, the stream you've been counting on to keep you alive.

Stumbling to the stream's edge, you want to just wade in and immerse yourself in the cooling water. As you plunge in, though, the realization hits you—there is no water! Finding yourself in the middle of a dry, rocky creek bed, it dawns on you that you had heard no sound of running water as you approached.

What could have happened? Where's the water?

Driven by your thirst, you head "upstream" to search for the problem. You know that the spring feeding the stream is not supposed to be all that far away. Staggering with weakness and fatigue, you move out.

Before long, your journey takes you around a hill and up a small valley. And there you find the problem. A short distance from where the water springs out of the hill, before it has had a chance to grow into a stream, someone has built a tall, solid dam. The flow of water down the hill, into the valley, and then into the familiar stream has been cut off.

And there you have a picture of what the Bible means when it says someone is under a curse. The flow of life-giving love and encouragement has been cut off. The person is without hope in a "dry" land.

Everyone and everything below the dam is now without water in a dry and barren land.

And there you have a picture of what the Bible means when it says someone is under a curse. The flow of life-giving love and encouragement has been cut off. The person is without hope in a "dry" land. It's a picture of life-giving water, dammed up and out of reach.

ACODs like me grew up under this kind of curse. The flow of love, support, and good modeling of a healthy marriage that should have been theirs from two parents while growing up was instead cut off. And they live with the effects of that curse every day of their lives.

Perhaps you're thinking that *curse* is too strong a word to use in describing the impact when parents divorce. Don't try telling that to Allison.

ALLISON'S STORY

As a young girl, Allison watched her parents fight constantly. Her mom took to drinking, and Allison became the de facto parent. Then one day her dad caught her mom in bed with another man, and the marriage was over.

Allison now found herself torn in half. She loved both parents, but any loyalty she showed toward one of them was seen by the other as treason. Her father sued for custody and got it, but it soon became clear that he was only using her to get revenge on her mother.

When Allison went to spend time with her mom, Mom's new boyfriend saw Allison as competition for Mom's time and attention. So he berated her, kept her under his thumb, and generally tried to make her life miserable.

At age 15, Allison came to the realization that the guidance and care she still desperately needed from loving parents were never going to be hers. She was on her own.

Not surprisingly, Allison developed a chronic mistrust of relationships. How could she believe anyone who claimed to love her (as her parents had)? How could she trust that others wouldn't try to manipulate her? And how was she supposed to get over the anger? She became convinced that if she ever did marry, she was doomed to repeat her parents' history.[1]

LIFE UNDER THE CURSE

Allison's case highlights what life under the curse of being an ACOD is like. Seeing her parents divorce makes an Allison wonder if any marriage can survive. Knowing that one of her parents committed infidelity makes her doubt that any marital partner can ultimately be trusted. Or maybe, she thinks, she herself will eventually follow her mother's example, even though that's the last thing she would intend right now.

In addition, if Allison marries but feels that her spouse doesn't understand her anxieties and so can't offer the support she needs, that, too, could become a source of constant tension in the home.

Statistically, studies have shown that children of divorce suffer from more depression, anxiety, low self-esteem, feelings of rejection, drug and alcohol abuse, delinquency, poor interpersonal relationships, and criminality than children from intact homes.[2] Sixty-five percent of children from divorced families will never build a good post-divorce relationship with their fathers. Thirty percent will be unable to develop a good post-divorce relationship with their mothers.[3]

As cited in the Introduction, ACODs are also at least two

to four times as likely to divorce as are adult children of intact homes. (And if both spouses come from divorced homes, the odds that they will divorce increase by *189* percent.[4])

> *The effects of divorce on childhood happiness may be more pronounced than the effects of death and may have deeper consequences on quality of life or emotional health.*

Statistics like these led one expert on the impact of divorce to write, "The effects of divorce on childhood happiness may be more pronounced than the effects of death and may have deeper consequences on quality of life or emotional health."[5]

As further evidence of the dramatic impact of parental divorce, consider the case of Frank and Betty. They met at college and became romantically and sexually involved. Then Betty discovered she was pregnant. They lived together until they graduated, then got married shortly afterward. But it was an unhappy marriage, marked by emotional abuse, constant fighting, and failure to resolve conflicts. After eight years of this, the relationship ended in divorce.

And not one bit of that was surprising.

Why? Because 20 years earlier, Frank's parents had met in college, become romantically involved, and gotten pregnant.

Then they had married and fought amid emotional abuse and unresolved conflict. Finally, after 10 years of contention, they had divorced.[6]

I could go on and on, but the picture is clear that children and adults whose parents divorce really are living under a curse. And the curse spreads from generation to generation until someone manages to break it and establish new patterns.

My Story

I, too, should have been one of those stories of living under the curse of divorce and the aching thirst it creates. My mother had been divorced once before meeting my father. My dad left my mom and divorced her when their three boys were all still under the age of three. He would go on to divorce twice more.

My own marriage, therefore, should have been a train wreck waiting to happen. To say I was a mess growing up would be putting the case mildly. As a young boy and then a teen, I longed for my dad's presence in my life. I was painfully aware—especially in my high school years—that other guys had dads who played catch with them, helped with their homework, attended their ball games to cheer them on, and then took them out for burgers afterward. *Am I really such a rotten kid,* I wondered, *that my dad couldn't stand to be here and do those things for me (and my brothers)?*

Like any child of divorce, I grew up asking all the "why" questions. I grew up with a model of marriage that said it's not permanent. I grew up with anger and frustration and got in trouble as a result. Early in dating, I broke off my relationships with girls whenever the girls started to get serious, because I didn't want to be hurt again.

By God's grace and with the help of a number of people, however, I beat the odds. I've been able to break the curse and avoid the wreck. I have a strong marriage, and I've worked hard at being a loving father to my two girls. I'm far from perfect in any way, but I have discovered that there's a way to "reverse the curse" and move toward the commitment and caring you and I really long for.

This book is designed to help you break the pattern, or cycle, of divorce as well—the curse you grew up with—and experience success in life and in marriage. To begin, let's look at some of the common manifestations of living under the curse in case you have any doubts about whether you're still under its spell.

QUESTIONS FOR REFLECTION
AND APPLICATION

1. How well can you relate, as an ACOD, to the word picture of thirsting for life-giving water, water that was cut off by your parents' divorce? Why?

2. In your own words, why are ACODs so prone to repeating their parents' mistakes and getting divorced themselves?

3. How important is it to you that I, though a fellow ACOD, am able to write from the experience of having built a lasting marriage? Why?

Chapter Two

MANIFESTATIONS OF THE CURSE, PART I

*Logically, of course, there's no way that
kids are responsible for their parents'
divorce. . . . But the heart can stubbornly
resist even what its own brain tells it, and
nowhere is this more true than in children
who eventually grow into ACODs.*

I've stated and illustrated that adult children of divorce are under a "curse," meaning they've grown up with life-giving elements "dammed up" or missing from their lives. Does that mean, however, that their parents were "evil" or purposely set out to create a deficit and life-shaping need in their lives? Of course not. As you'll see later in this book, my mother's steady, consistent love was a key to eventually reversing the curse in my life. Good people can and do divorce.

My mother didn't want my brothers and me to come up to a dry stream—but it happened, and it happens to ACODs today. Let's look at a number of reflections of the "curse" we can grow up under. What are some of the common negative effects, or manifestations, of this curse? Learning more about them can help you to better understand just how deeply you have been touched personally by the scourge of divorce in your family.

Gaining that understanding is vital. Why? *Because these manifestations, if left unchecked, can be the very things that will wreck your own marriage and continue the cycle of divorce in your family.*

From my own experience and research, I've identified 12 common manifestations of the curse. We'll take a brief look at each of them in these next three chapters. Then, in chapter 5, we'll see how to overcome these problems, *reverse the curse*, and build a strong and lasting marriage.

ISOLATION

People in prison are there because they've been convicted of doing something wrong, something illegal. They're sent to prison as punishment for their crimes, and prison life is harsh, indeed. But what do the guards do to punish inmates who cause trouble, who break the rules or get into fights and so earn the *strictest* treatment?

They put them into solitary confinement.

Prison officials know that short of physical torture, "solitary" is about the harshest thing they can do to a person. Oh, the prisoner might actually like it at first. He may feel safer, calmer, and glad to be away from other prisoners who were irritating or even threatening him. But that attitude soon changes.

Before long, the inmate starts to feel lonely. Whether he

realizes it or not, he was created for human contact. And the more time he spends in isolation, the more he will crave that contact. If he stays alone for weeks or months because he's considered dangerous to guards or other prisoners, he may begin to suffer serious consequences. One psychiatrist who studied inmates in solitary said that he saw effects ranging from "memory loss to severe anxiety to hallucinations to delusions and, under the severest cases of sensory deprivation, people go crazy."[1]

> *These manifestations, if left unchecked,*
> *can be the very things that will wreck*
> *your own marriage.*

All of that to say that isolation is punishment for human beings, pure and simple. There's no worse feeling than to feel that you're all alone in facing life and its struggles. Scripture affirms this when it says, "Two are better than one. . . . If one falls down, his friend can help him up. But pity the man who falls and has no one to help him up!"[2]

Yet, sadly, ACODs often put themselves in just such a prison of their own making. They withdraw from others emotionally, psychologically, and physically—even from their own spouses and children.

Why? They've been badly hurt by one or both of the most important people in their early lives (Mom and Dad), and they're afraid of being hurt badly again if they let someone else get close. Or they fear they may repeat the hurtful behaviors of their parents and end up harming loved ones themselves. Or because they grew up in homes of divorce, where they saw a powerful example of how *not* to build a healthy relationship, they may simply not know how to connect with other human beings in positive ways (my isolation of choice for years).

Of course, it's possible for the husband and wife to grow isolated from each other in any marriage. They get busy with work, hobbies, and social activities in their off hours. They may focus on their children, making less and less time for each other as the years go by. And nowadays, one or both may spend several hours a day surfing the Internet away from the family. But they don't usually set out to grow isolated.

With ACODs, however, while their isolation may not be consciously planned, it *is* intentional, for one or all of the reasons described above.

To get a better sense of whether you have a tendency to isolate yourself from friends and loved ones, answer the questions in the following self-test.

Isolation Self-Test:

- Whenever you have conflict with someone close to you, is your first impulse to "run away and hide"?

- Do you feel that it's emotionally dangerous to share your feelings, fears, and hopes with your spouse?
- Do you believe, even if you never say it aloud to anyone, that your friends and spouse will abandon you sooner or later?

If your answer to any one of those questions is *yes,* you probably have a tendency to isolate yourself. If your honest answer to any two or all three is *yes,* you almost certainly are prone to isolation.

UNHEALTHY FAMILY SECRETS

Another closely related problem commonly experienced by children of divorce is the tendency to be secretive about certain details of family life. Many times, children who grow up in broken homes learn that hiding embarrassing family information is better, in order to keep up appearances. In this case, the truism holds: Things are not always as they seem.

Certainly you know of some examples of "secrets" that are actually well-known, and kept with a wink and a nod. Al Capone, for example—the famous Chicago gangster from the 1920s—carried a business card that identified him as a used furniture dealer, even though everyone in the city knew his real occupation.

Then there are other secrets that are carefully hidden but

need to be revealed. There was, for instance, the case of the youth leader who was loved and respected by all in his parish, yet he turned out to be a child molester. Unfortunately, that terrible secret didn't come to light until after many children had been hurt.

Families are good at keeping unhealthy secrets, too. In one family, the wife and mother carried on an affair with a neighbor man. To say that she and her husband had a strange marriage would be an understatement, but the fact is that within their family, her relationship with the neighbor was known by all (though never discussed), including their four children. This secret was never revealed to the world outside the family, however, and so it and the affair persisted for years. (Eventually, the husband and wife did divorce.)

ACODs are highly prone to keeping unhealthy family secrets. And marital infidelity is just one of the dark secrets they may keep—secrets that likely contributed to their parents' breakup. Other all-too-common secrets include: the fact that their parents fought all the time. The fact that one parent is/was an alcoholic or drug abuser. The fact that one parent is/was a sexual abuser. The fact that one parent battered the other. The fact that the family struggled financially or was poor.

Why do ACODs tend to keep such terrible secrets? One obvious answer is shame. If a parent did something that led to divorce, like have an affair, there's naturally some embarrass-ment for all the family members. They understandably would just as soon not have the rest of the world be aware of what happened. It's the same situation when any loved one has done something to bring disgrace to the family.

> *The habit of keeping unhealthy*
> *secrets is usually learned*
> *from one or both parents.*

A second reason is that, like most habits, the habit of keep-ing unhealthy secrets is usually learned from one or both par-ents. Chances are that they tried to keep secret whatever problems they had, including those that led to their divorce. So their children learned that that's the way to handle problems, and the habit carried over into adulthood.

Finally, ACODs keep unhealthy secrets because they, themselves, have things to hide. They may have developed some of their parents' faults, or they may have problems of their own that they think they need to hide. So, in an attempt to protect their own reputation, they try to keep the truth buried away.

To gain a better understanding of whether you might have a tendency to keep unhealthy family secrets, answer the follow-ing questions:

Unhealthy Family Secrets Self-Test:

- Are you still today carrying some secret about your family of origin that you're unable to reveal to anyone else?
- Do you have any dark secrets of your own that you've never revealed to anyone?
- Do you have any person in your life—a spouse or a friend—with whom you can be completely candid?

If your answer to either of the first two questions is *yes*, you are in fact keeping unhealthy family secrets. And if your answer to the last question is *no*, you're going to have trouble overcoming this self-destructive habit.

FALSE GUILT

Another common manifestation of the curse of family divorce is false guilt. Many are the children who, when their parents split, come to believe that they (the children) are somehow responsible. And that false sense of guilt is often carried into adulthood.

My older brother, Joe, was not quite three years old when our parents divorced. He played no part in our dad's decision to walk out on the family, yet he quickly became convinced, even by age five or six, that he was somehow at fault. All our mom's reassurances that he was not to blame failed to budge him from this conviction. (And my grandmother's coolness toward "Little Joe" because he shared our father's name and looks didn't help at all.)

I noticed another good example of this manifestation recently (actually, while I was writing this) on television. Part of the backstory on USA Network's popular detective show *Monk* is that when Adrian Monk and his brother, Ambrose, were still young children, their father abandoned the boys and their mother. In the particular episode I was watching, *both* brothers finally admitted that for more than 30 years, each had felt responsible for their father's leaving.

Now, the show is fictional, but based on my personal experience and on talking with hundreds of ACODs over the years, I know that that story line was true to life. For more than 30 years, *each* could easily have been carrying that false load of guilt.

Logically, of course, children are not the responsible parties when it comes to their parents' divorce. The decision to end a marriage is made by the adults, and they alone are accountable for it. But the heart can stubbornly resist even what the brain tells it, and nowhere is this truer than in children who eventually grow into ACODs.

Why are ACODs so prone to false guilt, beginning with the tendency to feel responsible for their parents' divorce? The first reason is a deep feeling that when something as huge and terrible as your family's getting torn apart forever happens, *some-one* must be to blame. But the children, who love Mom *and* Dad and are trying desperately to cling to them both, don't want to blame their parents. They *need* to see their parents as still loving and caring for them, still willing to sacrifice for them.

And so someone else has to take the blame and be found guilty; more often than not, the children assign the role to themselves.

Not surprisingly, people who consider themselves guilty of something as awful as driving their parents apart tend to feel badly about themselves.

A second reason is that in the confused logic of children, if they're responsible for their parents' breakup—if their bad behavior or failure to somehow please the parent who left is what caused the divorce—then there's hope they can find a way to "make things right" and bring Mom and Dad back together.

If I can just be a good-enough boy so that Mom isn't always getting upset with me . . .

If I can get good-enough grades in school to convince Dad that I'm not stupid . . .

If I just take good-enough care of the house so that Mom will see how much help I could be if she came home . . .

If I can hit home runs and win all my baseball games and make Dad proud of me . . .

This is the kind of thinking that often dominates the minds of children of divorce. And thinking like this that is forged in the natural self-centeredness of childhood usually carries on into adulthood, as strong as the finest steel. It can also become generalized to feeling guilty about most anything that goes wrong.

Not surprisingly, people who consider themselves guilty of something as awful as driving their parents apart tend to feel badly about themselves. *I must be a terrible person to have destroyed my parents' marriage,* they figure. And, feeling that way, they also find it easy to consider themselves unworthy of love, undeserving of happiness.

The result: False guilt tends to drive ACODs to isolate themselves from others. Genuine guilt, in contrast—which results when you've actually, intentionally done something wrong—leads a person toward repentance and a life that changes for the better.

To assess whether you might have a tendency to struggle with false guilt, answer the following questions:

False Guilt Self-Test:

- Whenever anything goes wrong, is your first impulse to blame yourself?

- Even when an objective analysis of a negative situation shows that you're not at fault, do you still tend to think that you *must* be guilty somehow?
- Deep down, do you feel responsible for your parents' breakup?

If your answer to any one of those questions is *yes*, you probably have a tendency to feel false guilt. If your honest answer to any two or all three is *yes*, you almost certainly are prone to false guilt. And if your answer to the last question in particular is *yes*, you are *absolutely* experiencing false guilt.

Fear-Based Procrastination

Yet another common manifestation of the curse falling on ACODs is fear-based procrastination. Lots of people procrastinate, of course, and fear—especially of failure—is often the primary motivator. But ACODs are even more prone to putting things off than the norm.

Chad is a fortunate young man—he has found the woman of his dreams in Jenny. But even though he loves her dearly and likes to envision making a life and starting a family with her, he can't bring himself to actually ask Jenny to marry him. He's terrified of "taking the plunge" and making that huge commitment. Chad, not coincidentally, is an adult child of divorce.

Missy is a college sophomore, and it's time for her to

declare a major and commit to a particular course of study. But she finds herself frozen by fear and unable to make a choice. *What if I make the wrong decision and end up hating my major?* she reasons. *I'll have wasted a year or more of my life and thousands of dollars.* Missy, too, is a young adult child of divorce.

> *When you know from personal experience just how much failure can hurt, you're naturally reluctant to expose yourself to the possibility of such pain again—and far more so than someone who has never experienced a significant failure.*

Why is procrastination especially pronounced among ACODs? Let me count the ways! In a given case, it may be any one of the following reasons, or maybe a combination of some or all of them.

First, the most important relationship in the ACOD's life—the marriage of his or her parents—ended in bitterly painful failure. So the ACOD can find himself or herself afraid to start something lest it, too, end in painful failure. When you know from personal experience just how much failure can hurt, you're naturally reluctant to expose yourself to the possibility of such pain again—and far more so than someone who has never experienced a significant failure.

Along the same lines, just the whole idea of making a wholehearted commitment to something is likely to induce fear. Giving yourself completely to someone or some thing can be a mortifying prospect to the ACOD, yet it's also the key to fully enjoying a marriage relationship or most any other experience. Thus, the ACOD can find himself or herself in an agonizing dilemma.

The ACOD's fear of failure may also be rooted in concern for his or her parents. After all, they've already suffered greatly from the demise of their marriage. *If I try this [marriage, career, etc.] and fail,* the ACOD may reason, *it will be yet another bitter disappointment for Mom/Dad. I don't want to be the cause of more pain for them!*

Finally, if a young ACOD like Chad or Missy is struggling with various issues, doubts, and insecurities brought on by his or her parents' divorce, he or she may simply have a hard time concentrating on the task at hand and making steady progress. The lingering effects of the divorce may be like a persistent low-grade fever that saps strength and the will to work from a person with a mild infection.

Note that this tendency to procrastinate—like all the manifestations of the curse, really—often gets taken to one extreme or the other. An ACOD who's in the habit of procrastinating may well be one of the worst procrastinators around. Making decisions and getting things done can be a major, daily struggle for such a person.

At the other extreme, the ACOD may become almost fanatical in resisting the harmful patterns of his or her parents. A prime example is the child of an alcoholic who vows never to take a single drink—who won't even take cough syrup that contains a small amount of alcohol and who (typically) condemns even the most moderate alcohol consumption by others.

In the area of procrastination, some ACODs will reason, *My mom was always afraid to get help to stop my dad from beating her.* I'll *never hesitate to get the help I need.* Or, *I've seen how fear keeps my older sibling from making decisions, and I can understand why,* but I'm *not going to let the collapse of our parents' marriage keep* me *from doing what needs to get done. No, sir.*

To gain a better understanding of whether you might have a bent toward fear-based procrastination, answer the following questions:

Fear-Based Procrastination Self-Test:

- When you're facing a significant decision, do you tend to make it in a prudent but timely way, or do you put if off as long as possible, even well past the stated deadline?
- When you're given an assignment at work or elsewhere, are the first thoughts that enter your mind pictures of potential failure or pictures of potential success?

- When you think of making major personal commitments, is your predominant feeling one of joy or one of dread?

If you tend to put off decisions as long as you can, to automatically picture yourself failing at anything new, or to dread making personal commitments (such as marriage), you definitely have a problem with fear-based procrastination.

Living with the Curse

So far we've looked at four common manifestations of the curse of growing up in a home of divorce. In the next two chapters, we'll look at eight more. But don't give up hope! You *can* reverse the curse and break the cycle of divorce, as we'll see soon in chapter 5.

QUESTIONS FOR REFLECTION AND APPLICATION

1. Which of the manifestations of the curse described in this chapter do you think is potentially the most harmful? Why?

2. To which of these manifestations can you relate most personally? Why?

3. What impact is that manifestation having on your life as an individual? On your marriage (if you're already married)?

MANIFESTATIONS OF THE CURSE, PART II

*Whenever a marriage ends in divorce,
some seriously poor choices have been made
along the way, and kids always learn and usually
imitate what they've seen their parents do.*

As mentioned at the start of the preceding chapter, one or more of the common manifestations of the curse of growing up in a home of divorce may sink your own marriage if you're not careful. But perhaps you didn't relate to any of the four described in that chapter. Don't think you're out of the woods yet—here are four more typical traits of ACODs:

POOR CHOICES

Any person can make poor choices. Unfortunately, people from divorced homes can be emotionally pushed toward making some really bad choices. I know; I certainly have made my share.

From late grade school on into high school, my twin brother,

Jeff, and I chose to hang out with a rough group of guys. We were constantly getting into trouble, and it seemed that one prank led to another and another. The magnitude of our actions increased as well.

The summer before Jeff and I started high school, late one night, our "gang" decided to break into a darkened house. We thought it was empty, still under construction. But, as it turned out, the home was finished and occupied—the owners just weren't there at the time.

Well, to make a long story short, some people noticed what we were up to and called the police. We all got caught in the act. Fortunately for us, because we were juveniles, we were all let go with a stern warning and a ride home in a squad car. But that wasn't bad enough—I've never forgotten the look of shock and disappointment on our mother's face as Jeff and I climbed out of that police cruiser at two o'clock in the morning.

If our older brother, Joe, along with a few other key people, hadn't intervened and given us a push out of that group of friends (a story I'll tell elsewhere in the book), there's no telling what might have become of us. Two of those guys, who never left our "gang," later spent time in prison for drugs. Another actually died of an overdose. As Scripture says, "Bad company corrupts good character."[1]

One of the poor choices made by many ACODs today is living with someone without benefit of marriage. There's a certain logic to such a decision; after all, if your parents' divorce makes you question your own ability to build a lasting marriage, why not make a "trial run" with a willing partner?

> *ACODs are rebelling against the pain and sense of betrayal that they feel. They're still hurting from their parents' breakup, and they can strike out in destructive—sometimes self-destructive—choices and behaviors.*

Even apart from the moral issues surrounding cohabiting, however, it's a bad idea relationally and every other way. Research has shown that such couples are markedly less happy and less healthy than married couples. If cohabiting couples eventually marry, their likelihood of divorcing will be 46 percent higher than that of couples who marry without having first lived together.[2]

So why are ACODs prone to making poor choices? As with all the manifestations of the curse, the first and foremost reason is that this is what they've seen modeled by their parents. Whenever a marriage ends in divorce, even very good people have most likely made seriously poor choices along the way, and children learn and usually imitate what they've seen their parents do.

A second reason is that ACODs are rebelling against the

pain and sense of betrayal that they feel. They're still hurting from their parents' breakup, and they can strike out in destructive—sometimes self-destructive—choices and behaviors (or like me, turn anger at their situation into "legal" ways of hitting and hurting, from boxing to "knock them out cold" football).

A third reason can be that they're hungry for acceptance and a sense of belonging. Often feeling rejected by one (usually the noncustodial) parent or even both, they may be willing to do whatever is asked of them by someone who seems to offer love. If that someone is of the wrong sort, the result can be a whole string of bad decisions.

To help you discern whether you might have a problem with making poor choices, answer the following questions:

Poor Choices Self-Test:

- Looking back on your life as objectively as you can, do you see a pattern of making major decisions poorly?
- Have other people been seriously hurt by choices you've made?
- Based on your past decisions, do you feel confident about your ability to make good choices in the future?

If your honest answer to either of the first two questions is *yes*, and especially if you answer both in the affirmative, you've likely got a problem with making poor decisions. If you also respond *no* to the third question, you've certainly got an issue with poor choices.

FALSE STARTS

On a recent episode of the TV show *Inside the Actors Studio,* in which host James Lipton interviews successful actors, actresses, and directors, he began a new line of questioning with a famous actor by saying something like, "And now we come to a recurring theme on this program, the divorce of our guest's parents." And in fact it seems that there's news of another celebrity marriage breakdown every other week.

Some of these stars are known as much for their serial relationships as they are for their on-screen or on-stage work. Names like Madonna, Rosanne, Nicholas Cage, Angelina Jolie, Britney Spears, and Tom Cruise show up in the tabloids regularly. They've all been in multiple marriages and other pairings. And they're all ACODs.

But relationships are only one area where ACODs are prone to making false starts. You'll also see it in their attempts to break bad habits or establish good ones. The tendency shows up, too, in the multiple projects at home and at work that they start but somehow never finish.

These many new relationships, projects, and attempts at self-improvement are all always started with good intentions and high hopes. There's a genuine desire to succeed "this time." Yet time after time those hopes are dashed. A scripture says, "Hope deferred makes the heart sick,"[3] and that's a succinct, on-target description of what ACODs feel every time a false start comes to a bad end.

In the area of relationships, ACODs making false starts may be so desperate for love, acceptance, and security that they grab on to the first person who appears to offer them.

Why are ACODs so liable to make false starts? For one thing, as I've stated before, they've been badly hurt and are terribly afraid of being hurt again. But if they back out of a relationship before the other person has a chance to, they think (often subconsciously) they won't be hurt as badly. If they drop a project or an effort toward self-improvement, they avoid the pain of failure.

Of course, there's also the fact that ACODs making false starts are usually imitating their parents. Once again, it's a learned trait.

In the area of relationships, ACODs making false starts may be so desperate for love, acceptance, and security that they grab on to the first person who appears to offer them. When reality sets in, the love and acceptance may be only conditional and temporary, the security an illusion.

To get a better feel for your own tendency to make false starts, answer the following questions:

False Starts Self-Test:

- On a scale from 1 (poor) to 5 (excellent), how good have you been at following through on plans and commitments you've made?
- How confident are you of your ability to follow through in the future?
- Based on your experience, does the prospect of starting a new, close relationship fill you with expectation of a bright future or of another eventual heartbreak?

If your candid response to the first question is a 1, a 2, or even a 3, and if your answer to the second question is something like "Not very," you've likely got a problem with making false starts. If your answer to the last question is also an anticipation of heartbreak, you've definitely made a habit of false starts.

BROKEN COMMITMENTS

A close cousin to false starts is broken commitments. A false start often *ends* in a broken commitment. One example of this is the sad recent trend of more and more first marriages ending within the first five years. One writer, Pamela Paul, dubbed these "starter marriages," and she herself was divorced after less than a year of matrimony (and tries to say that's a good thing).

What do you suppose is the first risk factor for experiencing a "starter marriage" that Paul listed in her book on the subject? That's right, coming from a home where your parents divorced. Affirming what I've already said a number of times in this book, Paul points out that parents who divorced did not give their children role models for building and sustaining a healthy marriage. Instead, they modeled breaking the most important commitment in your life.

Another reason ACODs are especially prone to broken commitments is that they don't really like commitments. In their experience, commitments lead inevitably to disappointment and pain. Thus there's a tendency to make commitments only when they feel pressured into it and have no choice.

When they *do* make commitments, ACODs expect the other party to break them sooner or later. So, again, by breaking those commitments first themselves, they avoid (or at least lessen) the pain.

Are you likely to be a commitment breaker? To get an idea, answer the following:

Broken Commitments Self-Test:

- Do you have a pattern in your past of failing to follow through on commitments you've made?

- Have others told you they don't trust your promises?
- When you don't fulfill a commitment for whatever reason, do you tend to keep silent and hope people don't notice, perhaps also intentionally avoiding the person to whom you had made the pledge?

If you answer *yes* to even one of those questions, you've likely got a problem with breaking commitments. If you have to honestly say *yes* to two or all three, you're definitely finding it difficult to keep commitments.

BLAMING OTHERS

Have you ever known someone who, no matter what he does wrong, is always quick to point the finger of blame at someone else? He's never at fault. He could be caught red-handed doing something wrong and still claim that he's misunderstood and persecuted.

I know a man who was like this on the job. If someone pointed out that he spent too much time making personal phone calls, that person was insensitive and exaggerating to try to hurt him.

When this man failed to meet a deadline, it was because the project was more complicated than he had expected or the deadline wasn't reasonable.

When the man neglected to let his supervisor know that he

needed help to get his work done, the problem was that the supervisor had been "unavailable."

And when this man got nowhere in finding a mate, it was because none of the women he met were good enough to meet his standards. It was *their* fault things didn't work out.

ACODs genuinely feel powerless. After all, they couldn't keep the two most important people in their world together.

Some ACODs share this same tendency to blame others when things go wrong. When the problem is at work, a boss or co-workers or suppliers have to be at fault. When there are struggles in the marriage, the spouse or the in-laws are always to blame. If there are issues with their children, those children are being disrespectful and disobedient.

Why this propensity to blame others? For one thing, ACODs facing this aspect of the "curse" can genuinely feel powerless. After all, they couldn't keep the two most important people in their world together. They couldn't control what became of themselves after their parents' divorce—where they lived and whom they lived with and where they went to school. So they grew up feeling that the most vital things in life really are beyond their authority.

For another thing, others (Mom and/or Dad) caused their

greatest pain. It's easy and natural to assume, then, that others are also to blame when pain is experienced later in life.

Further, because of the pain that ACODs have experienced for years, they're understandably inclined to try to avoid more pain. And admitting you're to blame when you've done something wrong is painful. It hurts your pride. It also opens the door to still more pain in the form of a reprimand, a damaged relationship, or a loss of esteem in the eyes of someone you love.

Are you guilty of blaming others for your mistakes? To gain some insight into whether this is an issue for you, answer the following:

Blaming Others Self-Test:

- Looking back as objectively as you can, do you see a pattern of always pointing the finger at someone else when things go wrong?
- Have others ever told you that you seem to believe you can do nothing wrong?
- When was the last time that you accepted the blame, without argument, for something that wasn't done right or on time?

If your candid answer to the first or second question is *yes*, or if your answer to the last question is "A long time ago" or

"Never," you probably have a tendency to blame others. If you give those responses to two or all three of the questions, there's no doubt that blaming others is a concern for you.

LIVING WITH THE CURSE II

In this chapter and the last, we've now covered eight common manifestations of the curse of growing up in a home of divorce. I wish that this exhausted the list of common problems that I've seen and experienced myself. Sadly, that's not the case. In the next chapter, we'll look at the last four of these traits that are common to ACODs before turning to hope and help.

Remember, the good news is coming. Starting in chapter 5, we'll explore how to reverse the curse and break the cycle of divorce in your family.

Questions for Reflection and Application

1. Which of the manifestations of the curse described in this chapter do you think is potentially the most harmful? Why?

2. To which of these manifestations can you relate most personally? Why?

3. What impact is that manifestation having on your life as an individual? On your marriage (if you're already married)?

MANIFESTATIONS OF THE CURSE, PART III

*It's one thing to let another's words pass
in one ear and out the other. But to truly take
in and wrestle with that person's point of view,
desires, and expectations is tough stuff
for the already insecure.*

W e've now seen eight common manifestations of the curse of growing up in a home of divorce. These are the habits that can weaken the foundation of your own marriage if you don't do something to overcome them. And we're not done yet. In over 25 years of working with couples and singles—and in my own life—I've seen four more typical traits of ACODs that we need to explore, starting with one that can be among the most damaging:

SMOLDERING ANGER

It takes no great insight to observe that there are lots of angry people in the world today. From road rage on the highways to teens shooting up their schools to red-faced spouses screaming at each other in the middle of the night, anger seems to be all around us. Some of those people are simply out of control, but many have good reason for their rage. And among them are the adult children of divorce.

Jerry's parents divorced when he was still in grade school. He had seen and heard them argue all his life—often and at high volume. The peace never lasted long in their home. Still, when his parents went their separate ways, it came as quite a blow to Jerry.

The breakup of their home was only the start of Jerry's struggles, however. His father soon disappeared from his life altogether. Jerry felt betrayed and abandoned. How could his own dad turn his back on him completely?

Before long, Jerry was acting out in school. He grew surly at home, when he communicated at all. As time went by, still with no contact from his father, Jerry developed into an angry young man.

Children who go through their parents' divorce—at any age—also tend to get and remain angry at those parents, especially the one perceived as having pushed for the divorce.

As with the other manifestations of the curse, one reason ACODs are prone to anger is that they often saw it demonstrated by their parents as they were growing up. Marriages that end in divorce are often loud and angry long before the final split occurs. And children observing such behavior learn that that's how conflicts get handled.

Children who go through their parents' divorce—at any age—also tend to get and remain angry at those parents, especially the one perceived as having pushed for the divorce. That parent, more than anyone else (unless the ACOD is blaming himself or herself), is responsible for destroying the ACOD's sense of security and normalcy. Many ACODs have never gotten over that feeling of betrayal.

Of course, the parent who then moved out—who became far less of a presence in the child's life and maybe even disappeared altogether (like Jerry's father)—often became an object of anger as well. And in many cases, the ACOD has never forgiven that parent, never moved beyond the intense anger. How bad is that? In God's Word we're told: "But whoever hates his brother is in the darkness and walks around in the darkness; he does not know where he is going, because the darkness has blinded him."[1] In other words, our anger can push us deeper into that desert land of the "curse," further from the life-giving love and light we need.

This anger toward a parent can also become anger toward life in general because it hasn't treated the ACOD well or given him the "breaks" that other people get. *Why couldn't my parents have stayed together like So-and-So's?* the ACOD reasons. *I'm at least as good a person as her. Why did she get to have a parent at every soccer game, a dad to walk her down the aisle at her wedding?*

If you have any doubts about whether there's anger smoldering just beneath your own surface, answer these questions:

Smoldering Anger Self-Test:

- Do you have at least occasional feelings of anger or even hatred toward one or both of your parents?
- Do you get angry with others easily, often for no apparent reason?
- Has anyone close to you suggested that you have a problem with anger?
- Do you frequently get angry with yourself?

If your answer to one or two of those questions is *yes,* you likely have an issue with anger. If your honest response to three or all four is *yes,* you have a definite problem with unresolved anger.

NOT REALLY LISTENING

Another common trait of ACODs is not really listening to others. And failing to listen can damage relationships.

I think of Matt, the man who said that at the relatively young age of 34, he had already been married three times. Why so much marital failure so quickly? He claimed that it was because he was going bald and had been since high school. "My lack of hair is ruining my life!" he insisted. (Of course, if that were true, one could ask why all three women had married him in the first place.)

The fact is, however, that Matt was told repeatedly that he was obsessing over his hair and that it wasn't that big a deal to them (his wives). But he simply wouldn't listen. He had his mind made up, and that was all there was to it. The loving and reassuring words of three different wives were like water rolling off the proverbial duck's back.

Why does a failure to listen characterize so many ACODs? Reason number one is, again, parental example. Moms and dads in troubled marriages are often consumed with their own problems. To really listen to someone else requires shifting their focus to that other person. But when they're self-absorbed, wrapped up in their own troubles, such a shift usually doesn't happen.

Another reason is that, as stated earlier, ACODs can lack self-confidence. And really listening to someone else, especially someone with an opposing point of view or a different agenda, demands self-confidence and even courage. It's one thing to let another's words pass in one ear and out the other. But to truly take in and wrestle with that person's point of view, desires, and expectations is tough stuff for the already insecure.

To gauge your own propensity to not really listen, respond honestly to the following questions:

Not Really Listening Self-Test:

- Do people regularly have to make sure they have your attention before they start talking to you?
- Does your mind usually wander when others are talking to you?
- Do you often interrupt people who are speaking to you in order to interject your own point of view?
- Do you have trouble remembering the details of a conversation five minutes after it's over?

If your candid answer to one or two questions is *yes,* you could learn to listen better. If you say *yes* to three or all four questions, you have a major issue with not really listening.

UNENDING ARGUMENTS

He says black; she shouts white. He wants fish; she craves steak. He longs to buy the hot new sports car; she insists on the sensible used station wagon. He wants to arrive at social events 10 minutes early; she prefers to be fashionably late. And every time they lock horns, the arguing continues until one or both of them simply run out of energy.

It seems that no matter the subject, they're at opposite ends of the spectrum, and never the twain shall meet.

All couples disagree from time to time, of course. But ACODs are inclined to argue more, and in many cases they seem to be in perpetual discord with their spouses and/or others closest to them. Why this unpleasant and relationship-wrecking tendency?

We start, once again, with parental example. Growing up in a home that breaks apart because of divorce means being exposed to a lot of arguing. It's often frequent and loud arguing. And it's a pattern that leads, in the case of ACODs, to the death of the marriage.

> *All couples disagree from time to time, of course. But ACODs are inclined to argue more, and in many cases they seem to be in perpetual discord with their spouses and/or others closest to them.*

For ACODs, then, arguing loud and long is the normal way to handle disagreements. They often don't know how to resolve conflict in healthful ways. They've never learned to "fight" fairly and respectfully.

As noted earlier, ACODs also suffer from low self-esteem

and feelings of insecurity. This means, among other things, that they have an inordinate need to be "right" when they're at odds with someone else. If they can win the argument, they feel better about themselves, at least temporarily. If they lose, on the other hand, it only confirms their poor opinion of themselves.

Further, we've already looked in this chapter at how ACODs also tend to be angry and to not really listen to others. Those things being true, it's not surprising that they often end up in the middle of arguments. They were mad and inattentive to start with! And they're ticking off the people who live with them.

To get a handle on your own tendency to engage in endless arguments, answer these questions:

Unending Arguments Self-Test:

- When you have a difference of opinion with someone, is your first instinct to argue or to seek a meeting of the minds?
- Has anyone ever described you as "feisty" or said you're hard to get along with?
- Can you recall a day in the last two weeks when you *didn't* have at least one argument with someone?
- Based on your experience, would you say that you have good skills in resolving disagreements with those closest to you?

If your first instinct is to argue; if you answer *yes* to the second question, *no* to the third, and/or *no* to the last—these are indicators of a tendency to argue. If you give the negative response to two or more questions, this is a definite issue for you.

Seeing Only an Impersonal God

Late in the night of April 14, 1912, Third Officer Charles Victor Groves stood watch on the deck of his ship, the *Californian*, in the middle of the North Atlantic. His lumbering freighter was uneventfully going about its business of transoceanic commerce.

Then, out of the dark, came a huge, brilliantly lit apparition. Racing through the ocean at nearly full speed, the RMS *Titanic* quickly loomed larger and larger on the horizon. Even from a distance of 10 miles, the giant luxury liner on its maiden voyage from Southampton, England, to New York filled Groves with wonder.

As Groves watched in amazement, the *Titanic* seemed to fly by his ship. He remarked later, "I felt terribly small in comparison to its greatness." Neither Groves nor anyone else knew that the *Titanic* and all 2,209 souls aboard were only minutes from disaster.

As the *Titanic* flew by Groves that fateful night, its passengers and crew were seemingly unaware of his presence in the same patch of ocean. The few on board the mighty liner who noticed the *Californian* likely took little (if any) note of the nondescript cargo ship.

Many ACODs today can relate to what Third Officer Groves must have felt that evening. When they think of the mighty God of the universe, they see Him as big, impersonal, and vaguely aware of their existence at best. If He's involved in their lives at all, it's only as He "flies by" on His way to deal with matters that He considers more important.

From such painful experience, it's easy to conclude that God is uncaring or incapable of helping.

Why are ACODs prone to viewing God as cold and impersonal? Well, for starters, if they were old enough when it happened, they probably prayed to Him as their parents' marriage was breaking apart, imploring Him to keep them together. And what good did that do? Whatever else they might have prayed about in their lives, that had been their most important request, and all to no avail.

From such painful experience, it's easy to conclude that God is uncaring or incapable of helping. And if He couldn't or wouldn't help them and their families with that most urgent need, why trust that He would meet any other?

But thinking of God as uncaring or incapable can be

painful, too. If He doesn't care or can't help, we really are on our own, aren't we? So it becomes easier to think of Him as impersonal. That's just the way He is—like the *Titanic*, big and powerful and on His way to somewhere else.

That's a sad perspective because, as common sense as well as scientific studies have shown, people who believe in God and enjoy a personal, daily relationship with Him are happier and healthier, with a greater sense of purpose in life and hope for the future. They're better able to take on life's challenges and overcome its obstacles.

To gauge whether you might be looking at God as an impersonal being, answer the following questions:

Seeing Only an Impersonal God Self-Test:

- If someone asked you whether God answers prayer, would you say *yes* or *no*?
- Do you regularly pray to God about your own needs and desires?
- When your thoughts first turn to God, do you see Him as warm and personal or as cold and distant?
- Would you describe most of your experiences with God as positive or negative?

If you answer *no* to either of the first two questions, you likely view God as impersonal (no matter how you would describe your theology). If you candidly answer *no* to both, and if you also view Him as distant and/or consider your experiences with Him to be mostly negative, then you're certainly viewing Him as impersonal.

NOW FOR SOME GOOD NEWS

At last we've covered all 12 of the manifestations of the curse of being an ACOD that I see most often. If you're an ACOD, the chances are good that you can relate to one or more of them. But while these last three chapters have been a necessary if long stretch of "bad" news, we're now ready for some good news.

Starting in the next chapter, we'll begin to look at how to overcome the curse, including these troublesome traits so common to us ACODs. We'll see that there *is* hope for the future and that we *don't* have to repeat our parents' marital failures. We can learn, we can grow, and with God's help we can make better choices.

I trust you'll agree that that's good news, indeed.

Questions for Reflection and Application

1. Which of the manifestations of the curse described in this chapter do you think is potentially the most harmful? Why?

2. To which of these manifestations can you relate most personally? Why?

3. What impact is that manifestation having on your life as an individual? On your marriage (if you're already married)?

Chapter Five

REVERSING THE CURSE

*We need to know that we are loved with
a love that will not fade, will not weaken,
and will never abandon us. But as children of
divorce, life has made us afraid that such love
simply does not exist. And I'm here to tell
you that such love does exist.*

After reading through all those common manifestations of the curse of growing up in a home of divorce, you may be thinking that as an ACOD, you're doomed to fail at marriage. That certainly was the thinking of a woman named Carrie.

"I grew up watching my parents fight constantly," Carrie said. "They divorced when I was 15." And sure enough, Carrie's own marriage ended in a messy divorce after just six years.

Funny thing, though: Carrie has a sister, Cheryl. And even though Cheryl grew up in that same acrimonious environment and witnessed the same bitter divorce of their parents, she was still happily married, at 13 years and counting, at the time Carrie made her remarks.[1]

Two sisters—twins, even—both ACODs, yet entirely different outcomes in their own marriages. What does this tell us? Well, one obvious lesson is that while the ACOD curse presents a huge obstacle to marital success, it is by no means an insurmountable obstacle. It can be overcome.

In short, you can build a strong and lasting marriage despite your parents' divorce. You *can* break the cycle.

But how can you go about that? How can you defeat the odds, reverse the curse, and achieve something that eluded your own parents? That's what this chapter and the rest of this book will show you. And it begins with grasping and making daily use of a fundamental truth.

CHOOSE TO USE YOUR POWER

Coming out of a home of divorce, you've undoubtedly experienced a lot of pain and even trauma. You have pictures burned into your memory—of parents fighting with each other, yelling at each other, or maybe giving each other the cold, silent treatment. Perhaps you've even got pictures of your mom and dad physically abusing each other.

You are not a slave to your past. What happened to your parents' marriage does not have to happen to yours.

Maybe your pictures include one parent lying to the other, cheating on the other, expressing outright hatred to the other, or finally walking out on the other. And maybe your pictures include some of your parents' frustration and anger and pain being taken out on you and your brothers and sisters.

Whatever pictures circle around and around in your memory, and whatever ill effects they seem to have produced on your ability to sustain a healthy marriage, *the truth of the matter is that you have a choice about how you will respond.* You are not a slave to your past. What happened to your parents' marriage does not have to happen to yours.

You can pick a different outcome and make it your reality.

This power to choose how we will respond to life's challenges is one of the greatest of God's gifts to the human race. One of my favorite stories in this regard comes from the Bible; it's the true story of a young king named Josiah.

In ancient days, the kingdom of Israel was divided in two following the death of Solomon. In both the northern and southern kingdoms that resulted, the rulers who followed Solomon and his father, the great King David, were mostly evil. They turned their backs on the God of Abraham and led the people in worshiping idols. One of the worst was Manasseh, the grandfather of Josiah.

Here's part of what the Scriptures say about Manasseh: "In both courts of the temple of the LORD, he built altars to all the starry hosts. He sacrificed his own son in the fire, practiced sorcery and divination, and consulted mediums and spiritists. He did much evil in the eyes of the LORD, provoking him to anger."[2]

Not surprisingly, Manasseh's son who followed him on the throne, Amon, imitated his dad's terrible practices. Here's some of what we read about him: "He did evil in the eyes of the LORD, as his father Manasseh had done. He walked in all the ways of his father; he worshiped the idols his father had worshiped, and bowed down to them."[3]

After Amon was murdered, the people made Josiah king at the ripe old age of eight! Now, given the track record of his grandpa and his dad, we might have expected him to carry out a lot of religious depravity as well. Call it the curse of growing up in a really evil family! After all, that was the family history, the model he had seen since his earliest days, the only way of life he knew.

Instead, however, we read this about Josiah: "He did what was right in the eyes of the LORD and walked in all the ways of his father David, not turning aside to the right or to the left."[4]

I've always wondered who or what influenced Josiah to take such a different path from that of his granddad and father. Was it a devout nurse or tutor? Could it have been his mother? Perhaps it began with Josiah's seeing, even as a child, the destructive impact that idol worship had on the people and society of Judah.

Whatever the reason, Josiah *chose* to leapfrog, if you will, the evil example of his immediate forbears and identify instead with his ancestor David, called in Scripture "a man after God's own heart." Josiah refused to be bound by the corrupt beliefs and practices of the kings who preceded him. He recognized the better path—the path of truth and of national health and well-being—and resolutely set out to follow it.

This power to choose a better path despite growing up in a divorced family is yours as well. No matter what your background or your present circumstances, regardless of what life or other people have thrown at you, you can decide to think, speak, and act in ways that build up rather than tear down relationships.

You are not a slave to your family's past, any more than was Josiah.

Let me make this truth very practical for you. Let's suppose, for the sake of illustration, that as an ACOD, you often manifest the trait of smoldering anger. Whenever you and your spouse have any kind of disagreement, even over matters that seem trivial in retrospect, you're soon shouting and out of control.

You know what's wrong. You realize now, after reading chapter 4, that much of your simmering anger is rooted in your parents' divorce. But it's a deeply ingrained habit, and you've been like that ever since their breakup. Nevertheless, you can choose to change. You can choose to respond to conflict with your spouse in a more healthful way.

Certainly this isn't easy. You might feel powerless to make such a choice—and especially to follow through on it with any kind of consistency. Later in this chapter, we'll look at where the power comes from. But understand that reversing the curse begins with exercising your will and *choosing* to do so.

FACE YOUR FEARS

As we saw in chapters 2-4, we ACODs are prone to a lot of fears because of our painful experiences. They motivate many of the behaviors that we identified as manifestations of the curse of growing up in a home of divorce. To overcome those manifestations, then, we need to face our fears.

If one of our parents betrayed the other, we fear that our spouse will betray us. If one parent abandoned the other, we fear that our spouse will abandon us as well. And ultimately, since our parents failed at marriage, we're afraid that we will, too.

Or maybe we're afraid that *we're* destined to be the betrayer, the abandoner, and ultimately the one who causes the failure, as if it's in our genetic makeup or it's our destiny.

Melody was an ACOD with these kinds of fears. Only 13 when her parents divorced, she watched her father marry the woman with whom he'd had his affair. Then, just three years later, he divorced that woman as well. After that, he disappeared from Melody's life.

Twelve years later, though now "happily" married, Melody lived in fear that *this* man she loved would abandon her, too. Husband Cliff was a hard worker and devoted to their marriage, but he was also quiet and emotionally distant—just as her father had been.

Fear made Melody suspicious and contentious. Though Cliff had done nothing to earn her distrust, when he came home at night, she would grill him about where he had been, what he'd been doing, and with whom. And despite his innocence and his reassuring answers, she just couldn't shake the fear that he would one day abandon her—again, just like her dad.[5]

How do we overcome these fears? *First, we need to remember that fears grow in dark places, and they shrink in the light of day.* Our private imaginations can be such dark places. Talking openly with our spouses about our fears, along with our needs and expectations, can bring them into the light.

If Melody, for instance, would talk candidly with Cliff about her fear of abandonment and how it prompted her to conduct those nightly interrogations, it could lead to greater understanding and patience on both sides. He might agree to stay in touch throughout the day; she could agree to bite her tongue. And they could both agree to be gentle with each other when one of them slipped up on a given day.

Second, we can work to gain some objectivity about our spouse and our marriage. Rather than accept the notion that we're bound to end up like our parents, we can write out a list of the ways in which we and our spouse are *not* like our parents—especially in those faults that contributed to their divorce. Then we can write out a list of those ways in which our marriage is *not* like our parents' marriage, particularly in its troubled aspects.

It's a matter of reprogramming our thinking,
of focusing on—so we can build on—the
positives in our lives rather than the negatives
that grow out of a legacy of divorce.

Since most of us focus on people's shortcomings—our own as well as those of our spouse—it's also good to make another list of our (and perhaps our parents') strengths. One of the top items in that list should be our commitment to our spouse and to the relationship. Then we can make a list of our spouse's strengths and other positive attributes.

After we've made these lists, it's good to post them in prominent places in the home where we'll see them several times a day. The bathroom mirror, the refrigerator, and the computer screen are just some of the possibilities. And we can make multiple copies to post if need be.

Regularly refreshing our minds with these positive truths, just by glancing at our lists throughout the day, can help to chip away at and even counteract those fears. It's a matter of reprogramming our thinking, of focusing on—so we can build on—the positives in our lives rather than the negatives that grow out of a legacy of divorce.

Third, if we still struggle with our fears, we need to be willing to seek and accept help. A good friend who can hear us out and help us look at things more objectively can be a tremendous blessing. A professional counselor—one who shares our commitment to making our marriage work and be successful—can also offer valuable assistance.

Finally, spiritual resources can offer great comfort and even freedom from fear. I'll say more about this area in the last section of this chapter.

ADJUST BY TWO DEGREES

In overcoming the manifestations of the curse in our lives—choosing not to fail like our parents, facing our fears and the other principles discussed in this chapter—our natural human tendency is to want and think we *need* to make and see huge changes virtually overnight. For example, if our tendency for years has been to procrastinate, we'd like to be able to stop stalling and become super-productive the very next day.

In most cases, however, life doesn't work that way. Pastor and author Chuck Swindoll wrote a best-selling book a number of years ago called *Three Steps Forward, Two Steps Back,* and that's the way we usually make progress toward a positive goal. Or, as I like to put it, we need to aim to make just two-degree changes. Let me explain.

If you continue to make two-degree changes, you will change where you end up.

On a compass, two degrees isn't much of a change in direction. When you consider that a normal right or left turn onto a perpendicular street is a 90-degree change, a turn of only two degrees seems inconsequential. It's hardly worth noticing.

But if you continue to make two-degree changes over an extended time and distance, the ultimate result will be a huge change in where you end up.[6]

The potential impact of small changes got impressed unforgettably on my mind one summer day in a cramped, sticky-hot 727, sitting on the tarmac at the airport in Austin, Texas. My work requires a lot of air travel, so I'm well acquainted with long delays at the ticket counter, long delays at the security checkpoint, long delays at the gate waiting for the plane to come in, long delays . . . well, you get the picture.

On this memorable day, though, my flight had actually been pushed away from the gate on schedule. *I might even get home on time*, I mused. But no. After taxiing a mere 500 yards from the terminal, heading toward the runway, we suddenly came to a stop. The pilot came on the intercom and announced, "Folks, we just found out we have a paperwork issue we have to iron out. We'll be stopping here for a few minutes."

As I said, I know all about air travel delays. So I realized that the phrase "a few minutes" could mean "anytime between now and when your youngest child graduates from college, falls in love, gets married, and gives birth to your new grandkid." And I normally stay calm and use the time in that aluminum tube to read, write, or do correspondence on my laptop. But when my battery ran out, and after sitting next to this stranger for what was becoming a very long time, I decided to strike up a conversation with my seatmate.

It turned out that he was an engineer from the Houston area. Jumping to a logical conclusion, I asked if he worked for one of the oil companies.

"No, I work for NASA," he replied.

Well, I'm sure that in the 60 minutes that followed, he came to deeply regret having told me that. As a kid growing up in the Apollo period of manned space flight, culminating in the first walk on the moon by Neil Armstrong and Buzz Aldrin, I had dreamed of becoming an astronaut. Now here I was, talking with a genuine rocket scientist who could answer all my questions about space flight!

And ask I did. To his credit, the man patiently responded, even telling me some behind-the-scenes stories that I took in like a kid watching his favorite Saturday-morning cartoon. I was having a great time!

Then I asked a question that I considered simple but that the engineer saw marked me as a real novice. "What are the tolerances you build into the trajectory for a moon flight?" I said. "For example, after you blast off, could you be off target just a little, maybe two degrees, and not have it be such a huge problem?"

The man knew the basic answer but wanted to show me exactly how crazy my idea was. So he whipped out his briefcase and pulled out his handheld calculator, which looked like a Cray supercomputer stuffed into a box the size of a paperback novel. I could just hear my laptop saying, "Wow, that's what I want to be when I grow up!"

The man punched in the "very approximate" distance from the earth to the moon of 225,740 miles, depending—of course—on the time of year and the apogee of the moon's orbit around us. Then his fingers flew over the keyboard for a bit as he plugged in the variables in some equation that I would never understand in a million years.

Finally he announced, "Be just two degrees off after

blastoff, and roughly taking the time and distance traveled into account, and you'll not only miss your point of orbital entry around the moon, but you'll actually miss the moon by about 11,121 miles." And he turned the calculator toward me so I could see he was not making this up.

Now, we've already established that I'm no rocket scientist, but even I knew that 11,000 miles and change was quite a lot! Just a two-degree error in your flight path and you could find yourself on the way to Mars instead of to the moon. Or, to state it differently in terms that apply to you and me every day, just a slight difference in direction, over time, can make a huge difference in where you end up.

This is as true in a positive sense as it is in a negative. And it gives us a great deal of hope in overcoming the manifestations of the curse.

Let's suppose, as before, that you really struggle with procrastination. Instead of doing the things you need to every day, you tend to sit for hours in front of the TV after coming home from work. Before you know it, it's time to go to bed each night, and the work remains undone. You recognize that this is a problem, and you figure you really ought to quit watching TV altogether, starting tonight.

But that's not realistic, is it? Your habit of wasting the night in front of the TV is deeply ingrained. Besides, you have some favorite shows that you really enjoy and are going to want to watch. My suggestion: Start by making a two-degree change.

Let's say you're watching four hours of TV each night. Don't expect to cut that to zero tomorrow. But how about cutting just one half-hour show out of that lineup? Surely there's at least one sitcom that you're watching more out of habit than because you really enjoy it. Turn off the TV just for that half hour, and load the dishwasher, pay some bills, or take care of some other need during that time.

Try that for a week. It's a small change, nothing too drastic, but it's movement in the right direction. And it's a lot easier to tell yourself, *I can do without one sitcom per night,* than it is to think, *I have to quit watching TV!*

At the end of that week, if you weren't able to turn the TV off for half an hour at least four or five nights, try again for another week. The more you try, the easier it will get. And as soon as you *are* able to skip that sitcom more often than not for a week, look at your viewing schedule again and see if there isn't *another* half hour of TV that you could live without each night.

Again, take your time with this. Some nights you'll fail, but more and more nights you'll succeed. That small change in direction, after a while, will add up to a major change in your procrastination-by-television habit.

I once read that we tend to *overestimate* how much we can

accomplish in the short run and *underestimate* how much we can accomplish in the long run. And I believe that that's very true. But by making just two-degree changes in our bad habits, we can eventually make major progress in overcoming them. (I'll say more about the value of two-degree changes in chapter 7.)

START WITH ONE

Consistent with the idea of making two-degree changes, there's also great wisdom in focusing on overcoming just one manifestation of the curse at a time. If you're like most of us ACODs, you probably struggle with several of the marks of the curse. Ultimately, you'd like to conquer all of them, and preferably all at once.

But just as we don't generally make drastic improvements overnight in an area that's been troubling us for years, so we also are liable to be more sorry than successful if we try to tackle multiple manifestations simultaneously. Better results usually come from focusing on one thing at a time.

> *Better results usually come from focusing on one thing at a time.*

As I mentioned earlier, one of my "issues" from growing up in a home of divorce was anger. I continued to struggle with it (and other things) well into adulthood. And one of the ways it came out was that after my two daughters were born, when I'd get upset with them, I would point my finger at them while scolding them. It was irritating and even scary to them, definitely not a healthy habit.

Now, I could have tried to tell myself, "I'm never, ever going to get angry at my children again. Starting tomorrow, I'm always going to be calm and kind, even when they willfully disobey me or Cindy!" And that resolve, frankly, would have lasted less than a day.

Fortunately, it occurred to me that the atmosphere would start to improve between me and my girls if I could just break that habit of pointing at them menacingly while reprimanding them. So I came up with a "small" but practical way of breaking the habit. I gathered them around me one day and announced, "Girls, Daddy wants to stop pointing at you in anger when he's talking to you. So here's what we're going to do that's going to help me do that: From now on, every time I point my finger at you when I'm angry, I'm going to pay you one dollar on the spot!"

As you might imagine, Kari and Laura thought that was a great idea. Visions of kid-sized riches started dancing in their heads.

For my part, I didn't relish the idea of "throwing away" my money, so I was privately determined not to pay out a single buck. And sure enough, I suddenly found myself much more aware of when I started to point at them. That's not to say, however, that my wallet stayed shut. In fact, over the next three weeks, I paid out almost $20 in singles!

The good news is that by the end of those three weeks, I had become so attuned to when I was about to point at them that I was finally catching myself and stopping before I raised the dreaded finger. The girls had mixed feelings about that.

The even better news is that breaking that bad habit with this simple approach had a ripple effect. First, it helped me to get my anger under control quickly when I became upset with my daughters. In order not to point, I had to stop and think about what I was about to do and why. That proved to be enough of a pause for me to get a grip on myself.

Second, I found myself increasingly able to control my anger in all situations, not just when the girls did something bothersome. I was more in tune with my emotions and more aware of what it felt like to start losing control of them.

And third, I discovered that growing in this one area helped me immensely in other problem areas as well. The effort to improve in controlling my anger weakened the hold of other bad habits, too. Talk about unexpected bonuses!

SEEK ACCOUNTABILITY

What do groups that help people with habitual, even addictive behaviors—groups like Alcoholics Anonymous and Gamblers

Anonymous—have in common as a key to success? Account-ability. They have found that sometimes, when a person is sorely tempted to give in to an urge, the *only* thing that keeps that person from surrendering is the knowledge that in a few days, someone whom he or she respects and does not want to disappoint is going to ask, "Did you give in to the urge this week?"

I've found the same to be true in my own life—on a simple scale, with my daughters, as described in the preceding section—in my work as a counselor, and in working with men through the group called Promise Keepers. I can't count the number of times that a man has said to me, "I was so tempted to _____ this past week"—whatever the bad habit with which he was struggling. "The only way I kept from giving in was thinking about how I would see _____"—me or someone else to whom he had made himself accountable—"in a few days and knowing he was going to ask the question and not let me fake my way through a lie."

Done right, with someone you trust and who will respect your need for confidentiality, accountability can be a powerful tool in your efforts to overcome the manifestations of the curse and build a strong marriage.

Do you tend to blame others for everything that goes wrong in your life, especially your spouse? An accountability partner can help you look at things more objectively.

Do you tend to break your commitments and make multiple false starts toward real change? Your accountability partner can call you on that and give you the nudge you need to stay the course.

> *In short, someone to whom you're willing to make yourself truly accountable can be a great asset in dealing with any of the manifestations of the curse.*

Do you tend to stuff your negative feelings and keep secrets? An accountability partner can draw out how you really feel and help you face up to what you're thinking and doing.

In short, someone to whom you're willing to make yourself truly accountable can be a great asset in dealing with *any* of the manifestations of the curse. As suggested above, this person needs to be someone you can trust to have your best interests at heart and to protect your privacy. It also needs to be someone to whom you're willing to spill your guts. And it needs to be a person who will ask you the tough questions about how you handled your problem area(s) since you last met, and who won't let you dance around the truth when you answer.

Who might be a good candidate to become your accountability partner? It could be a friend, a member of your extended family, a clergy person, or a counselor. But wherever you can find the right individual, I encourage you to avail yourself of this tremendous source of help.

GET PROFESSIONAL HELP
WHEN NEEDED

With a doctorate in counseling, it would be easy for me to just sit on that side of the room, wearing my psychologist sweater and dispensing advice to others. However, one of the best decisions Cindy and I ever made was to seek a "coach," or counselor, for a yearly tune-up. As the scripture says, "Where there is no guidance the people fall, but in a abundance of counselors there is victory."[7]

It started when my father was dying and we had to make a lot of decisions about all the issues surrounding that relationship (such as whether he should move into our home). Cindy suggested that we sit down and talk to someone. Knowing this would cost money, I pressed her to see if she was serious. She was. So I called a friend who is a counselor with a Ph.D. We scheduled three sessions to meet with him and talk through, as a couple, how to face the situation with my father. Frankly, I thought there really wasn't much to talk about and we'd finish in one session. However, after three sessions, Cindy was ready to sign up for three more weeks of coaching!

That started something that we have done, almost without

exception, for 20 years: meeting once a year for three sessions with a trained counselor to talk through whatever issues life has thrown at us that year. My travel schedule was the focus one year, along with the struggles of raising junior high kids and an unexpected job change. Later, it would be the death of my mother and the loss of Cindy's parents in the same year.

> *Especially when you're dealing with a really tough issue, problem, or cycle, and you don't seem to be making progress on your own, a trained professional can be a great help.*

In other words, at least for my part, I will die long before I run out of issues to talk through with a trained "coach." I'm purposely using the word *coach* instead of *counselor*. In most cases that's what people, including ACODs, need: some strategic, short, positive, future-oriented coaching by a trained counselor—not years and years of in-depth meetings with a therapist.

Cindy and I would both agree that those almost yearly meetings with Dr. Retts have been a tremendous help to our marriage—and to reversing the curse. Am I saying that everyone should go to counseling? Absolutely not. However, I am saying that everyone should, as the scripture above says, seek guidance. Especially when you're dealing with a really tough issue, problem, or cycle, and you don't seem to be making progress on your own, a trained professional can be a great help.

Choose a counselor with care, though. Pick a person with outstanding faith and experience. If you can, get a referral from someone you know has been helped significantly with issues like your own. You can also get help from Focus on the Family in locating a good counselor in your area. Just call 1-800-AFAMILY.

Rest in God

Finally and most importantly, the power to do everything positive that I've discussed in this book comes by drawing on the love and power of God. All the other suggestions I've made are important, and you can follow them on your own to one extent or another, depending on your level of motivation and your strength of willpower. *But the greatest power to make lasting change comes from gaining an accurate understanding of God and His love for you, and then letting Him work in and through you.*

Imagine that I tell you about the joys of the Apple iPod and how convenient it makes it to enjoy your favorite music wherever you go. Then I describe all the steps needed to download your tunes, locate the songs you want to play, and crank up the volume. But while giving you all that help, I neglect to mention this thing called *the battery* and the role it plays and the whys and hows of keeping it charged. Your iPod will soon run out of power and become nothing more than an expensive decoration on your shelf.

Well, for me to give you the other keys to overcoming the manifestations of the curse without mentioning God would be just like that. Those other keys are important, even vital, but the most necessary truth is that God is the greatest difference-maker in individual lives and in marriages.

First, then, we need to get that better understanding of God and how He wants to relate to us. He's *not* impersonal. He's *not* unconcerned. He *hasn't* turned His back on us even though people (e.g., our parents) have hurt us or let us down with their decisions.

Here are just a few of the truths we find about God and how He feels about us in the Scriptures: "Are not two sparrows sold for a penny? Yet not one of them will fall to the ground apart from the will of your Father [God]. And even the very hairs of your head are all numbered. So don't be afraid; you are worth more than many sparrows."[8]

"Cast all your anxiety on him [God] because he cares for you."[9]

"But because of his great love for us, God, who is rich in mercy . . ."[10]

"And so we know and rely on the love God has for us. God is love. Whoever lives in love lives in God, and God in him."[11]

The psalmist wrote, "Answer me, O LORD, out of the goodness of your love; in your great mercy turn to me."[12]

"You are forgiving and good, O LORD, abounding in love to all who call to you."[13]

"For the LORD is good and his love endures forever."[14]

And then there is perhaps the best-known verse in the entire New Testament: "For God so loved the world that he gave his one and only Son, that whoever believes in him shall not perish but have eternal life."[15]

So God not only loves us—loves *you*—but He loves us enough to invite us to cast our anxieties on Him, to forgive us, and to make an unfathomable sacrifice in order to offer us eternal life. *This* is how God feels about us.

If this is a new concept to you, or if you just have trouble believing it, I encourage you to review and meditate on these truths several times a day. Dog-ear this page, and come back to it over and over. Write these passages on notecards and carry them with you so you can reread them as you go about your daily activities. Let these truths sink deep into your heart and mind.

You see, all the manifestations of the curse grow out of the fact that every human being needs—craves, can't live joyfully without—unconditional love. We *need* to know that we are loved with a love that will not fade, will not weaken, and will never abandon us. But as children of divorce, life has made us afraid that such love simply does not exist. And I'm here to tell you that such love *does* exist. It's real, and it comes from the God who made us. We must grasp and hold on to this truth and never let go—just as He will never let go of us.

When we come to accept the reality of God's love, to allow Him to fill that gaping hole in our hearts, that love will start to reverse the curse for us. Understanding that we are loved with a love that will never desert us, never violate our trust, and never disappoint us, we will feel less and less of a need to be angry, to argue, to procrastinate, to make poor choices in a desperate search for love, and so on.

I'm not saying all this will happen overnight—remember the principle of two-degree changes. But over time, as we learn to bask in God's love, we will tend less and less to live like someone under a curse.

> *When we embrace God's love*
> *and ask for His help, He responds.*

At the same time, not only does God's *love* help to reverse the curse, but so also does His *power.* Let me explain.

When we embrace God's love and ask for His help, He responds. Remember the scripture above in which we're invited to cast our anxieties on Him. In another scripture, we see a historical example of His love and power combining to thwart a literal curse.

The people of Israel, having escaped from bondage in Egypt, were about to enter the land promised to them by God. Understandably, the people already living there (known as Ammonites and Moabites) were not keen on that idea. But they also had heard the stories about Israel's prior conquests en route from Egypt, so their leaders decided they needed more help in defeating Israel's encroachment than their armies alone could provide. They needed surefire spiritual help.

So these leaders sent for a man named Balaam. Balaam had a reputation for being connected to God. If Balaam gave someone a blessing, that person usually got blessed by God. In the same way, if Balaam spoke a curse against someone, that person normally got cursed by God. Curse Israel for us, these leaders told Balaam, and we'll pay you handsomely.

Well, Balaam went and tried to curse Israel all right—four different times. But each time, he found himself able to say only those things that God wanted him to say about Israel, which were all blessings! The leaders, and especially King Balak of Moab, got mightily upset with Balaam and told him to pack up and go home.

Later Moses, the leader of Israel, reminded the people of that incident, and he explained just what had happened: "They hired Balaam . . . to pronounce a curse on you. However, the

LORD your God would not listen to Balaam but *turned the curse into a blessing for you,* because the LORD your God loves you."[16]

Isn't that amazing? What Balak and his fellow leaders had meant to be a curse against Israel, God instead—by His power and because of His love—turned into a blessing.

Likewise God both wants to *and* can *turn the curse under which we ACODs have lived into a blessing.*

He loves us—He loves *you*—enough to do that for us.

What's more, God's power can strengthen us internally to do what we know we should in a given situation. When we don't want to turn off the TV; when we're about to start another argument; when we want to blame someone else for something that went wrong—we can ask for and receive His help to do the healthier thing instead.

We read in Scripture, "For it is God who works in you to will and to act according to his good purpose."[17] He strengthens us both in our *desire* to do what's right and in our *ability* to actually get up and do it.

And another passage tells us, "I can do everything through him [God] who gives me strength."[18] Whatever we know is good and right, something that He would want us to do, He will empower us to do.

The question is, then, will you turn to God and draw on His love and power to help you reverse the curse in your life?

Reversing the Curse and Breaking the Cycle

To break the cycle of divorce in our families, to build strong marriages of our own, we need to reverse the curse that we've been living under as children of divorce. Using the principles in this chapter—and especially drawing upon the love and power of God—will do so much to help us reach that goal.

As we'll see in the next chapter, having an example to follow can also be a tremendous asset in our quest for strong and lasting marriages.

QUESTIONS FOR REFLECTION AND APPLICATION

1. Which of the principles, or strategies, offered in this chapter do you think will be most immediately helpful to you? Why?

2. What action can you take today to begin to put that strategy into practice?

3. How would you describe your relationship with God? Are you regularly seeking His help, or are you trying to live (and make your marriage work, if you're married) on your own?

THE POWER OF AN EXAMPLE

I went from hoping that surely I could somehow be more successful at marriage than my parents to firmly believing that this would be the case. Despite living under the curse of parental divorce, I could and would have a solid marriage.

T hroughout this book, I've made the point that one of the ways in which adult children of divorce (ACODs) are under a curse is that the primary example they've seen of marriage—in many cases the *only* example—is an example of failure. The only picture they have is a picture that says marriage just doesn't last.

Conversely, adult children of healthy intact families enjoy the advantage of experiencing that marital commitment can and does last. They enjoy the blessing of *knowing*, from first-hand experience, that even when there's conflict in a home, the relationship can survive and even thrive rather than fall apart.

As an ACOD myself, I should have been cursed by the lack of a good marriage model. But by the grace of God, I was instead blessed with not just one but two powerful examples of love and lasting commitment. Let me tell you about them, and then we'll explore the specifics of how such examples can make a dramatic impact in an ACOD's life.

My Story

The first outstanding model of love and commitment that God gave me was my mom, Zoa Trent. Since she divorced twice and was a single parent for most of my life, you might wonder how she helped me to believe in the permanence of marriage. Here's how:

My mom was, in a word, a *great* mom. She loved me and my two brothers unconditionally, and we—okay, I especially—put that love to the test many times. When I acted out in anger over my father's refusal to be a part of our lives, she never gave up on me, never accepted the idea that I was beyond redemption.

When, as teens, my twin brother and I would come home after a night of carousing with our friends, she would be up and waiting for us. Because of her warmth and acceptance, we'd be eager to jump onto her bed, one on each side of her, and tell her where we'd been and what we were thinking.

Sometimes on the weekends, we got home late at night. But every time we asked if it were still okay to come into her room, she'd say, "I'll always have time to sleep, but I won't always have you boys to talk to."

As you'll see in the next chapter of this book, my mom also

went *way* out of her comfort zone to meet her boys' needs. She took small steps to help, and she took big steps to the best of her abilities. Over the years, I've met a lot of dedicated and wonderful single moms, but none tops Zoa Trent in my estimation.

Now, the reason you need to know all that is this: Though her own two marriages failed, my mom never stopped believing in the institution of marriage as God designed it. Especially after she became a Christian (which happened after her divorces), she developed the deep conviction that God wants marriage to last a lifetime and that with His help, it's not only possible but normal.

And because of the way she modeled love and commitment to us, my brothers and I had no trouble trusting her when she talked about such things.

> *Without an example of marital success to look at regularly, hope is hard to come by.*

We weren't seeing a healthy marriage lived out before us every day. But we were seeing the kind of rock-solid, utterly dependable, and tenacious love that she told us would one day characterize our marriages. We were seeing the kind of commitment that says, "You will always be mine, and I will always be yours, no matter what." And so we had confidence that we could also enjoy such commitment to and with our wives one day.

The second great model God gave me was a man named Doug Barram. Doug was the Young Life leader at our high school, so I began to see him my freshman year. My twin brother and I were football players, and Doug was one of the few people who didn't just come to games but also to *practices*. He'd yell out words of encouragement as we ran plays or trotted past him on our way to the locker room. (He was a big man at six-foot-four and about 225 pounds, and he had played football himself.)

Before long, Doug had learned my name and seemed genuinely excited to see me each time we met. He was always open to talking about whatever we teens wanted to discuss, and he invited us to hang out at his house, with his family.

In Doug's home, for the first time I saw a strong marriage up close. The man obviously adored his wife; you could see it in the way he looked at her, spoke to her, kissed her, and helped her. And you could see that she felt the same about him. This was the husband I wanted to be in due time.

He also clearly loved his children—playing with them, wrestling with them, talking with them, praying with them, and tucking them in bed at night. So here, too, was the model of a great father that I needed to see.

Watching Doug Barram relate to his family, I was like a giant sponge, soaking it all in. This was the family life for which I had yearned and about which I had only heard before.

I loved being around them so much that I cut his grass every week just to have an excuse to be there. (I would have painted his house and put on a new roof, too, if it had needed them.)

In this model, my mom's words about what marriage should be came to life. She had provided a vision; Doug and his family put flesh on the dream. Between the two, I formed my expectations for the kind of marriage relationship that I would one day build.

WHAT A MODEL PROVIDES

If you're an ACOD, just what are the benefits you could gain from finding a good marriage model (or model couple)—benefits great enough to make the search worth your time and effort? My models gave me four things primarily, and they summarize the benefits pretty well.

First, they gave me hope that marital commitment can *endure for a lifetime.* If your only family experience has been that marriage doesn't last, that conflicts lead inevitably to the death of the relationship, you need hope. You need some reason to believe that things can be different in the future, different for you and your spouse.

Without an example of marital success to look at regularly, however, such hope will be hard to come by. Your frame of reference will still be confined to scenes of failure.

A model like Doug Barram expanded my frame of reference. I saw that failed marriages aren't the only kind. That marriage can not only survive but even be great. That what my mom had said about how marital commitment is supposed to last a lifetime is true.

Second, my models gave me the expectation that commitment will *endure for a lifetime.* Once you have the hope that marriage *can* endure, you need to progress to the expectation that it *will* endure. Though you've previously seen only marital failure, marital health and thriving need to become your new idea of normal.

The impact of parental divorce on the expectations of ACODs is so powerful that one researcher was led to observe that young people today tend to enter marriage "in a profound state of cluelessness."

Again, however, the encouragement and example of my mom, plus the strong relationship of Doug Barram and his wife, eventually developed a realistically positive expectation in me. I went from hoping that surely I could somehow be more successful at marriage than my parents to firmly believing that this *would* be the case. Despite living under the curse of parental divorce, I could and would have a solid marriage.

Third, my models gave me examples of healthful ways to relate—daily habits that build up a marriage. Relationships often founder because, for various reasons, the people in them simply stop doing the positive things that keep the tie strong—

things like helping each other. Saying "I love you." Putting an encouraging arm around a discouraged loved one's shoulder. Deferring to the other's desires as often as possible.

"We are mesmerized by the romantic idea of marriage and blinded to the reality," wrote Gen X author Pamela Paul. "We are sold on Cinderella, not on how uncomfortable wearing glass slippers for the next 50 years might be."[1]

In other words, we forget how much hard and consistent work it takes to live "happily ever after."

> *We are sold on Cinderella, not on how uncomfortable wearing glass slippers for the next 50 years might be.*

Here again, though, my mom and Doug Barram came through for me. Over years of watching Doug and his wife, Loretta, I saw love put into action. I saw my mom regularly putting her children's needs ahead of her own. And I saw Doug helping his wife around the house and with their children and telling her "I love you" in various ways. Even when making a request at dinner like "Please pass the carrots," his love and respect for her shone through.

Fourth, my models gave me examples of how to resolve conflicts without destroying the relationship. Conflict is inevitable, and ACODs tend to think it inevitably leads to divorce. But in healthy marriages, husband and wife find ways to work out their differences and grow even closer together as a result.

In these four significant ways, my mom and Doug Barram showed me, despite my handicaps as an ACOD, that I could have a good marriage. They shaped my hopes and expectations, and they gave me the practical skills for building strong, lasting relationships. Their examples have played a key part in the making of my marriage.

FINDING A GOOD MODEL

If you're an ACOD and you haven't been blessed with positive examples like the two I enjoyed, where can you find them? Here are some possibilities:

First, ask God to bring individuals and couples into your life who will model healthy marriage for you. He cares so much for you, and He wants to provide for your every need, including this one (see 1 Peter 5:7).

Second, look around you. Perhaps among your relatives there's a couple who stand out as having a strong, stable marriage. You might also find such a person or couple in your circle of friends, among your neighbors, or even at your place of work. The good news is that though your experience has led you to think of marriage as a relationship that's likely to fail, there are, in fact, many solid marriages all around you.

Third, one of the best places to look is in your local church. Although Christian or other religiously based marriages aren't perfect, they are typically among the strongest you'll find.

The next few times you're in church, look around you before and after the service. You may well see some couples who demonstrate obvious love and respect for each other and might be good to observe further. Talk to your pastor and explain what you need; he might even be able to recommend a couple who would invite you to spend time with them, watch how they relate, and ask whatever questions you might have.

In short, you're looking for another Doug Barram family. You want a couple who will mentor you in how to have a healthy marriage.

GOOD MODELS—DON'T LEAVE HOME WITHOUT THEM

As an ACOD, you face tough odds in trying to experience a strong, lasting marriage. You'll recall that at the start of this book, I compared it to being asked to paint a scene (of a desert in bloom) that you'd never observed, in person or in picture. Next to impossible, right?

Well, what good models can do for you is provide the picture. They can show you what the scene is supposed to look like. They can prove that this scene is not just a pleasant figment of someone's imagination, not just a nice fantasy that's far removed from the realities of daily life.

Good and even great marriages do exist. Find one or two and soak in what they look like and how they work. And let the conviction begin to grow in your heart that you, too, can experience such a lasting and fulfilling relationship.

QUESTIONS FOR REFLECTION AND APPLICATION

1. Do you already have at least one positive model of commitment and unconditional love in your life?

2. If you still need such an example, where might you find it?

3. Which of the benefits of a strong role model might prove most helpful to you? Why?

STEPPING OUT
OF THE TRAILER

*If I say I'm going to do something,
and I know that my accountability partner
is going to ask me about it soon, and he's not
going to accept any excuses for failing to do it,
I'm a lot more motivated to follow through.*

In chapter 5, I wrote of the fact that we have the power of choice, a power that we have to exercise for good if we're to break the cycle of divorce. That principle is so important that I want to expand on it in this chapter.

The reason this is such a big deal is that making the right choice *and acting on it,* when we've been used to making the wrong choice, takes us way out of our comfort zone. And we human beings just *hate* to move out of our comfort zones. But we have to be willing to do that, consistently, for the rest of our lives, if we're going to build and maintain healthy marriages.

Let me tell you the story of a woman who was willing to move way out of her comfort zone and, in the process, helped to break the cycle of divorce for her three sons.

MY MOM, MY HERO

After my father deserted our family, leaving my mom as the single parent to three boys, she pushed herself out of her comfort zone in so many ways to meet our needs and bless us that I can't begin to count them. But one in particular stands out in my memory.

My mom was not the outdoorsy type. In fact, that statement would draw peals of laughter from most members of my family. Given the choice, she would prefer the amenities of city life any day. Furthermore, she didn't have much money in those years to feed and care for a family of four. No one would have blamed her if, when she got a little extra cash, she spent it on her own comfort and pleasure.

I tell you those things so you can appreciate what happened one weekend day early in my childhood. Mom had gone out that morning in our pathetic, old Ford Falcon. She hadn't told us where she was going. When she came home a little later, the Falcon was towing a tired, worn, teardrop trailer. Inside, we soon discovered there were some of the basic tools of camping: a lamp, a propane stove, a tent, and some flashlights—all well used.

We were going camping! We boys were thrilled at the prospect. Mom tried hard to convince us she was, too, and we believed her at the time. She'd managed to save a few extra dollars, and rather than spend them on herself, she had spent them on something she knew we'd love.

Off we went, that same day, to Rocky Point, Mexico, for our first camping adventure. Now, understand that Mom knew nothing about camping, and of course neither did us boys. But that didn't stop us or even diminish our enthusiasm.

Once we got to our campsite on the Mexican coast, however, reality set in. We couldn't get the stove to work. Ditto for the lamp. We were clueless about setting up a tent. Even the flashlights were dying. We went to sleep a little cold and a little hungry. The next morning found us huddled together in the trailer, second-guessing just how great camping was supposed to be. I can only imagine what Mom was thinking, but I imagine it included a longing for her soft, warm bed back in Phoenix.

> *It all began with a mom who made a choice to do something that would help her sons to cope with the curse of divorce— something that required her willingness to step way out of her comfort zone.*

Then the Cholla Bay Camping Club showed up. This was a group of kindred spirits who loved camping together and did so regularly. They quickly set up camp and got a nice, warm fire going—something we had been unable to do. Soon one of the men came over and invited us to join them for coffee and hot chocolate. They didn't have to ask twice!

After we were warmed up, those pro campers showed us how to fire up the stove and cook on it. How to light the lantern. How to pitch a tent. They even scrounged up replacement batteries for our flashlights.

At the finish of that weekend, as our time there drew to a close and everyone prepared to go home, the members of Cholla Bay Camping invited us—the only single-parent family in the group—to join their club. For the rest of my growing-up years, we went with them once a month to Rocky Point. It was great fun, great learning, with plenty of positive male role models for us boys.

And it all began with a mom who made a choice to do something that would help her sons to cope with the curse of divorce— something that required her willingness to step way out of her comfort zone.

You might say that she was willing to step out of the trailer to break the curse.

WHY IT'S SO TOUGH

All human beings are creatures of habit. We take comfort in the familiar. Even when we know change would probably be good for us, we still struggle to take that first step out of the trailer. We're leaving the known for the unknown, and that's scary.

In my book *Heart Shift*, I describe nine reasons why all people struggle to take that first step out of the trailer. These range from lack of time to fear of failure to fear of losing what we already have, and so on. And these are understandable reasons for hesitating to initiate change.

For ACODs, the difficulty in taking that first step is magnified. We're even more fearful, more suspicious, less optimistic, and less trusting than the norm. Even when we know what we're leaving behind is bad, it's still so hard to step into the unknown.

Let's suppose, for instance, that you have the habit—a manifestation of the curse—of blaming others for everything that goes wrong. This book has brought home to you the reality that that's just not the case. You need to start accepting responsibility for—at the very least—your *response* to the bad things that have happened to you.

> *Even when we know what we're leaving behind is bad, it's still so hard to step into the unknown.*

Again, any normal person will struggle to step out of the trailer and start accepting that responsibility. It's uncomfortable. It's nice to deflect blame to a scapegoat. But for you as an ACOD, it's even harder than usual to accept blame.

For one thing, it will require admitting that you've been wrong about some important things, like how much of your current unhappiness is the fault of the parent who "caused" the divorce or who left the home after the breakup. It will also require forgiving the parent who hurt you the most—and believe me, I know how tough that can be. You might even need to ask for his forgiveness for blaming him unjustly all these years.

If all that weren't hard enough, stepping out of the trailer to stop blaming others will require you to look honestly at your own shortcomings. How much of your pain have you brought on yourself through your attitudes, words, and actions? Which of your own habits make it difficult for you to build healthy relationships?

Answering such questions won't be easy. But it will be necessary.

TWO-DEGREE CHANGES, PART II

The good news, as I first explained in chapter 5, is that you don't need to—and shouldn't try to—make huge changes overnight. Small changes in the right direction can add up over time to major course corrections.

This point was made hilariously in the film *What About Bob?*, starring Bill Murray as the title character—a man with some serious psychological issues. His therapist, played by Richard Dreyfuss, advocated an approach that he called "baby steps," which was very much akin to the idea of two-degree changes. (In fact, the therapist had written a book called *Baby Steps*. He gave Bob a copy and added the cost to his bill.)

The film's humor comes from Bob's naïve, bumbling attempts to make those baby steps of progress. The situation gets even funnier when lovable but annoying Bob invites himself into the middle of the therapist's family summer vacation.

Though the movie plays Bob's efforts for laughs, he does make a certain amount of progress over the course of the film. And as we've already seen, the concept itself is entirely valid. So the question then becomes, what might it look like to step out of the trailer, to make the first two-degree change in overcoming whichever of the manifestations of the curse is causing you the most trouble? Let's take a look at some possibilities.

Suppose you have a tendency to isolate yourself. Your first step might be to ask your spouse out for a date. If you withdraw physically in your own home, you might make a point of sitting with your spouse one evening while you both read or watch TV together.

If you struggle with false guilt, your first step might be to simply write on a note card, "I am not to blame for my parents' divorce." Then carry that card with you and look at it several times throughout the day. Reading it aloud to yourself would be another small step in the right direction.

If you've been keeping unhealthy family secrets, a safe first step would be to write them out on a piece of paper. Then destroy the paper if you feel you must, but write them out again the next day and the next. (Eventually, as you ask God to give you the strength, you'll want to show that paper to someone you can trust.)

If you're prone to fear-based procrastination, your first step could be to break down some task you need to do into small, manageable pieces. Just write out the stages. A simple example could be paying your bills. You might write, "Gather bills, checkbook, and pen. Open first bill, see how much is owed, and write the check. Put the check and return portion of the bill into the return envelope, close and seal. Attach stamp." And so on. (Next you'll tackle that first stage, which may give you the momentum to go on to the second.)

If you've been making poor choices, your first step might be to ask yourself, "What lessons should I have learned from my previous mistakes?" Or you might ask, "What mistakes have I made that I definitely do *not* want to repeat?"

Likewise if you're in the habit of making false starts, you might ask yourself, "Why did those attempts to do something good end so badly? What lessons have I learned?"

If breaking commitments is a problem for you, you might start asking God to give you wisdom about which commitments you should and shouldn't make, which promises you can and can't keep. To encourage yourself, you might also write out and review regularly, "I am a person of integrity. I make wise commitments and keep my promises."

If you've tended to blame others for everything bad in your life, your first step could be to make a list of the people you blame most often and the things for which you blame them. (Your next step might then be to analyze, as best you can, how much of the problem is what each of those people said or did and how much is the way in which you've chosen to respond to those words or actions.)

If you struggle with smoldering anger, you might start by identifying some way in which you give evidence of that anger—like me pointing my finger at my daughters. (Then, also like me, you could think of some way to make yourself vividly aware of what you're doing and begin to get control of that behavior.)

Is not really listening to others your problem? Your first step out of the trailer could be to force yourself to wait until the other person finishes speaking a thought before you reply. In other words, no more cutting off the other person in mid-sentence. Or you might start briefly repeating back to the other person what you understood her to say, before you give your response. ("If I heard you correctly, Joan, you're concerned about . . .")

Suppose you're prone to launch into an argument at the drop of a hat. You could start forcing yourself—again, asking for God's help—to monitor your feelings in a given conversation or situation. As you do this, you'll probably begin to notice what triggers your emotions, your feeling of defensiveness, or your sense of needing to disagree. Another first step might be to ask yourself, before you respond, "*Why* does this other person think or feel that way?"

Finally, if your struggle is with seeing God only as impersonal and unconcerned about you and your pain, a great first step would be to turn back to those scriptures in the last section of chapter 5—the ones that speak of His love and care for you. Then write them out on small cards that you can carry and review throughout the day. Another first step would be to write out a list of all the *good* things God has put in your life. Go back and add to it over a period of several days. Then review it every day. It isn't difficult to start making small but important changes. (Please see my book *The Two-Degree Difference* if this idea of two-degree changes has grabbed your heart.)

The Value of Making Yourself Accountable

Earlier in this book, I spoke of the value of making yourself accountable to a trusted person for the changes you're trying to accomplish. But the message bears repeating here.

As I said earlier in this chapter, even small, first steps in the right direction can be hard to pull off. But the task can be made immensely easier if you're not trying to do it alone. Your spouse, a sibling, a close friend, a counselor—someone you can trust to have your best interests at heart and to respect your privacy—can be a great asset in taking the baby steps that eventually lead to major improvements in your life.

Such an ally can provide encouragement when you're frustrated or disappointed. He or she can also help you analyze situations more objectively than you can on your own. And, if you'll allow it, this person can hold you accountable for making your two-degree course corrections along the way.

I'll say it again: There's great power that comes from knowing that in a day or two or three, somebody you trust and respect is going to ask you the tough questions. "Did you stop to ask *why* your wife was saying something you found irritating before launching into an argument?" "Did you look at your schedule and analyze what you could realistically do before making any new commitments this week?" "Did you point in anger at your girls this week? If you did, did you pay them a dollar on the spot?" "Did you take that first step toward preparing your tax returns this week—did you make your list of all the documentation you'll need to gather?"

You get the picture. If I say I'm going to do something, and I know that my accountability partner is going to ask me about it soon, and he's not going to accept any excuses for my failing to do it, I'm a lot more motivated to follow through.

Knowing you'll be called to account for something you know you ought to do may not be the most noble reason to do it, but it works.

I urge you, therefore, to find yourself a good accountability partner even before you step out of the trailer to start overcoming those tendencies that weaken your ability to sustain a strong marriage. Finding such a person is itself not a small step, but it will greatly enhance your chances of making all your subsequent steps successful.

TRUSTING THAT GOD WILL "SHOW UP"

Back in chapter 5, I referred to that time in ancient history when the people of Israel were moving from slavery in Egypt into the land that God had promised to give them. Well, in another part of the story, those people were about to take a *big* step; they were about to cross the Jordan River from east to west, into that land flowing with milk and honey.

Life and health imply movement. When we make the choice to move, God shows up.

Moses, their leader, knew he was about to die and would not cross the river with the rest of the nation. So to prepare the people for going on without him, he reminded them of all that God had done for them and of the laws He had provided to guide them in daily living. Then, near the end of his lengthy message, he spoke these words: "This day I call heaven and earth as witnesses against you that I have set before you life and death, blessings and curses. Now choose life . . ."[1]

In the Hebrew language in which that biblical book of Deuteronomy was originally written, the word translated *life* means "movement." That's one of the ways that we check on whether something is alive, isn't it—whether or not it's moving under its own power. Life and health imply movement.

In the same manner as God through Moses challenged Israel to choose life—to move forward into that land of promise, obeying His laws—He also challenges us ACODs today. He calls us to choose life, to start moving in small but steady steps to break the cycle of divorce in our lives.

When we make that choice, day by day and even moment by moment, the amazing thing is that God "shows up" on our behalf. He strengthens us to do those things that we need to do, whether it's looking at ourselves and our lives more honestly, speaking words of blessing rather than blasting, taking that next small step in the right direction, or whatever the need of the moment may be.

What's more, God does those things that we need but that we can't do for ourselves. In Israel's case, He parted the waters of the Jordan at flood stage so the people could cross over on dry land. He gave them victory after victory over superior forces. He made the thick and fortified walls of a mighty city fall to the ground. Scripture tells us that on one occasion, He even made the sun stand still long enough for Israel to bring a late-day battle to a successful conclusion!

In our case, God can change hearts. For example, I don't know about you, but I simply can't find it in myself to fully forgive someone who has hurt me badly. God, however, has worked that willingness in my heart many times.

He can also strengthen and enable an arthritis-crippled single mom named Zoa Trent, who wanted to model commitment to her sons, to be there for them 24/7, taking them camping in their formative years and speaking calmly and lovingly to them in their rebellious teen years. (*Zoa*, by the way, is Greek for *life*, and no one was ever better named.) She chose life for herself and her boys, and her attitude in spite of her physical pain was always "Let's get moving!"

God can also open doors to overcoming the curse in our lives. I wrote in chapter 6 about Doug Barram, the man who introduced me to God in my high school years and who showed me what it means to be a husband and a father. I wasn't looking for such a man; I didn't even know I needed that kind of loving example. But God knew what I needed and brought Doug into my life.

After I had gotten to know Doug, and I had also finally met my dad—who had lived no more than 20 miles away all those years while I was growing up and had never made contact of any kind—I took a close look at the two examples they provided of how to live a life. And I chose life and I chose blessing. I vowed that when the time came, with God's help, I would be Doug Barram and not my father to my own wife and children.

Whatever it is that you need to overcome the curse and break the cycle of divorce in your life, I encourage you to choose life. To step out of the trailer. To call on God for His help. And to look expectantly for Him to show up, empowering you to do your part and to do *for* you those things that are beyond your grasp.

He's a big God. A miracle-working God. And He loves *you.*

QUESTIONS FOR REFLECTION
AND APPLICATION

1. What will be required of you if you're to step out of the trailer and deal with your most troublesome manifestation of the curse?

2. What might be your first two-degree change in addressing that manifestation?

3. To whom could you make yourself accountable for taking your first steps in the right direction?

4. What do you need God to do for you that you can't do for yourself?

TOUCHING FUTURE GENERATIONS

Children may not ask you tough questions about how you're living (but then again, they might), but never forget that they're watching you, listening to you, and learning from your every move, every day.

As human beings caught up in the daily routines of life, we tend to wonder sometimes if what we're doing really makes much difference. In the working world, are we just cogs in the business machine? If we have children, do they recognize all that we do for them, much less appreciate it? Will all of our hopes and efforts have any lasting impact?

Well, I'm living proof that (a) divorce is a generational curse and, therefore, (b) if you can break the cycle of divorce, you do so not only for yourself, but also for your children, your grandchildren, and generations even in the distant future.

How's that for lasting impact?

The reason I'm evidence of both *a* and *b* is that I had a terrific mom who broke the cycle of divorce for my brothers and me. By all accounts, our marriages and our lives generally should have been deeply troubled. That we've fared so well is tribute to the fact that our mother chose life and blessing and passed these on to us.

The principle she taught was that marriage is supposed to be a permanent, lifetime commitment.

Let me remind you, through the words of Elizabeth Marquardt (herself an ACOD) in her book *Between Two Worlds*, of the common experience of many of our fellow ACODs: "Our parents' divorce is linked to our higher rates of depression, suicidal attempts and thoughts, health problems, childhood sexual abuse, school dropout, failure to attend college, arrests, addiction, teen pregnancy, and more. . . . Some of us continue to struggle with the scars left from our parents' divorce: we have a harder time finishing school, getting and keeping jobs, maintaining relationships, and having lasting marriages."[1]

Again, the fact that my brothers and I avoided most of that heartache is a credit to our mom. Let me tell you more about her.

A SINGLE MOM'S LEGACY

My mom was divorced twice before she discovered and embraced God's love for her. After that, as she read the Bible and learned more of His principles for living, she not only applied them to her own life but also taught them to her sons. And one of those was that marriage is supposed to be a permanent, lifetime commitment.

As I pointed out earlier, it might have sounded strange to hear a twice-divorced woman teaching the permanence of marriage. But her commitment to us was so rock-solid, so clearly unconditional, that we never doubted the truth of what she was saying or the fact that such a relationship was possible. After all, she modeled that kind of love every day.

She went to all our football games, baseball games, and wrestling matches. She washed sweat, blood, and grass stains out of our uniforms, even with severely arthritic hands. She took us to the library, where we roamed free while she looked for books to help her in forging a career and fighting a crippling illness. She prayed for us every day, often with tears in her eyes during Jeff's and my turbulent teen years.

She taught us how to be men, and not just men but *gentlemen*. She always expected the best of us and forgave us the worst. She couldn't tie a necktie or button a coat—she couldn't even spank us when we misbehaved. But when she put her hand gently on mine and spoke her concern for my conduct, her eyes pierced my soul and I wanted desperately never to disappoint her again. (Of course, I often did.)

She never spoke negatively of our father, either. She never

blamed him for deserting us, never bad-mouthed him for our financial struggles.

Do you begin to see how we beat the odds?

*We've seen the kinds of attitudes, words,
and behaviors that destroy a marriage.
We're struggling even now to overcome
those same tendencies.*

Far from dropping out of school, my twin brother, Jeff, and I both earned Ph.D.'s. He became a cancer researcher; I became a counselor, speaker, and writer. Our older brother, Joe, trains Realtors to be outstanding at serving others.

As for our marriages, I've been married for 26 years and counting to Cindy, the finest woman I've ever known besides my mom. Jeff's wife, Dee, struggles with multiple sclerosis, yet they've loved each other dearly for more than 30 years. Joe did get divorced (after 20 years), but he has grown both spiritually and in general maturity since then. He's now 10 years and counting into a solid second marriage, applying what Mom taught us all.

THE IMPACT WE CAN HAVE

When we break the cycle of divorce and build strong and stable marriages, we spare our own children from the heartache and pain of divorce, and we greatly improve the chances that their children will likewise be spared. We pass on blessings rather than a curse. We help them to be much more healthy and happy than children of divorce.

As ACODs, because we've experienced the curse and are choosing every day to reverse it, we can also give our children the benefit of our own painful past. We've seen the kinds of attitudes, words, and behaviors that destroy a marriage. We're struggling even now to overcome those same tendencies. With age-appropriate, loving candor, we can guide our children in building healthy relationships and avoiding destructive habits.

By the way we treat our spouses and children, we can also be for them the kind of model that my mom and Doug Barram were for me. We can show them:

- how to communicate openly and honestly.
- how to be proactive and take initiative.
- how to make good choices.
- how to put the needs of others before our own.
- how to make and keep commitments.
- how to ask for and offer forgiveness.
- and how to relate to, and draw strength from, a loving God.

Besides providing this kind of example to our own children and other family members (e.g., nieces and nephews), we might also look for other children of divorce who, like me with

Doug, would benefit from such a living illustration of healthy adulthood. These might be friends of our children, children on the same sports teams as our children, or children in our places of worship.

THE GOAL

Elizabeth Marquardt captures the goal well here: "Many of us dream of a whole family, unbroken by divorce—a family where our children never even think about the concept of home because they blessedly take it for granted. . . . In my early twenties I wasn't able to imagine a future for myself, but now I see a future bright with hope.

"[I]t's not enough to love our children. As hard as I know it can be, we parents must also do our best to love and forgive *each other*, every day. . . . We do this so that we can sustain unbroken families that last a lifetime, not just for the sake of our own happiness, but for theirs."[2]

*Ask yourself every day, "What kind of
legacy will I leave to my children?"*

To that perspective I would only add that our own power to love and forgive is limited; the real power comes from God. But the well-being of our children and of theirs *is* the ultimate goal.

Let me encourage you, then, to ask yourself every day, "What kind of legacy am I leaving to my children?" Or, if you don't have children, "Based on how I'm currently dealing with the effects of being an adult child of divorce, what impact am I having on those around me? If nieces, nephews, or other young people are observing me, what lessons are they learning from my example?"

When you think about it, this is another form of accountability. Children may not ask you tough questions about how you're living (but then again, they might), but never forget that they're watching you, listening to you, and learning from your every move, every day.

In short, your life and how you handle the tough realities of being an ACOD *will* have an impact on future generations. The only question is what kind of impact it will be.

And the answer to that is up to you.

QUESTIONS FOR REFLECTION AND APPLICATION

1. Besides yourself and your spouse, whose future might be most affected by the success or failure of your marriage? Your own child? A sibling? Future children?

2. What does my mom's story tell you about the potential impact of a parent, even a single parent, on a child of divorce?

3. In your own words, what do you hope will be your legacy in the area of personal relationships?

Chapter Nine

IF YOU'VE
ALREADY BEEN
DIVORCED

*We need to learn from the past, but we must
not become slaves to it. It's today and tomorrow
that we can make positive changes, today and
tomorrow that God has given us to do those
things that will build a strong marriage.*

P erhaps you've read to this point—or you skipped ahead when you saw this chapter on the contents page—and you're thinking, *This idea of breaking the cycle of divorce sounds well and good, but I'm already divorced. Realistically, isn't it too late for me? I'm right in the middle of the cycle of divorce, just like my parents before me.*

The resounding answer is that *no*, it's not too late for you. And *yes*, you can still break the cycle of divorce.

Whatever has happened to you in the past, or whatever poor choices you have made yourself, you can start fresh today. With God's help, you can put the past behind you and start taking wise, healthful steps in the right direction. It has become a cliché, but today truly is the first day of the rest of your life, and your future can be so much brighter than your past.

THE GOD OF SECOND CHANCES

The biblical book of Luke, chapter 15, includes one of the most remarkable stories in all of Scripture. It's a story that Jesus told and that seems to be aimed straight at people who need a second chance—people just like you and me.

Whatever has happened to you in the past,
or whatever poor choices you have made
yourself, you can start fresh today.

The story centers on a young man, his older brother, and, in the middle of it all, their father. The young man—let's call him Tom—was feeling frisky, as our parents used to say—eager to get out and "see the world," to indulge every appetite. To finance his adventure, he went to his dad and said, "Father, give me my share of the estate."[1]

Now, since a family estate didn't normally get divided up until the patriarch died, Tom was essentially saying, "Dad, I wish you were dead. But give me my share of the family money without making me wait for that."

When the father graciously granted his request in spite of the disrespect, "the younger son got together all he had."[2] He packed up all his possessions, because he was leaving and had no intention of ever coming back. He was making a total break with his dad (and the rest of the family).

Then Tom "set off for a distant country."[3] His goal: Put as much distance as possible between himself and his father. That was not only true physically, but it was also true morally and spiritually. As soon as this reckless jet-setter landed in that faraway land, he began to spend his money as if there were no tomorrow, on "wild living" (booze, fast women, and who knows what else).

Much to the young man's disappointment, however, tomorrow did come, and quickly. Soon all the money was gone, along with all his new, good-time friends. Now Tom was penniless, homeless, friendless, and still clueless.

It didn't help that his adopted homeland went into a severe economic depression at the same time. Jobs were hard to come by. The only work Tom could land was tending a herd of pigs—and even the pigs were eating better than him!

What was he to do? He had cut all ties with his family, made a mockery of his father's values. The dictionary of the day could have put his photo next to the entry for "poor choices." At this point, he didn't deserve anything from his dad except contempt and condemnation.

And yet . . .

Our young playboy knew enough about his father to have a glimmer of hope that maybe, just maybe, Dad would show enough mercy to let him be a household servant. To be reinstated as a son—that was beyond comprehension. But the servants ate pretty well in his father's home, and that looked good compared to sharing seed pods with the sows.

So off young Tom went, heading toward Dad's estate, rehearsing the speech that he hoped would gain him admittance to the servants' quarters. Desperate for some kind of second chance. No other options if he caught his father in a bad mood.

Now here's where the story starts to get interesting for those of us who need a second chance.

While Tom was still some distance from the home spread, just a speck on the horizon, his father saw him. Which means that Dad was *looking* for him. A glance in the right direction wouldn't have done the trick; Dad was *straining* to see the young man. Maybe he had climbed the tallest hill on the estate; maybe he had built a tower on that tallest hill. He *longed* to see his son again, and he refused to give up hope that the young man would return someday.

So when he saw Tom, Dad took off running toward him. When he got to him, he threw his arms around Tom and kissed him. Tom started into his humble-pie speech, but Dad cut him off. "Quick! Bring the best robe and put it on him," he told the servants. "Put a ring on his finger and sandals on his feet. Bring the fattened calf and kill it. Let's have a feast and celebrate."[4]

And then came words that had to have struck Tom to the core of his being. "For this son of mine was dead and is alive again," Dad said. "He was lost and is found."[5]

The father said so much with those few words. He said that

despite Tom's rebellion, despite his despising all that his dad stood for, and despite his throwing away half the family fortune, all was forgiven. And regardless of what the young man deserved—a servant's position at best—Dad was restoring him to the full status and privileges of "son-hood."

Tom was back in the family, being given a clean slate and a fresh start. Not only that, but Dad was even throwing a party in his honor to welcome him home!

The great news for us is that Jesus, in telling this story, was clearly saying that this gracious, loving, forgiving, second-chance-providing father is a true picture of God, the heavenly Father. God, Jesus said, loves us, longs to be with us, and forgives us just like the dad in the story.

And no matter how badly we may have blown it in life, even turning our backs on Him, He's ready to run in our direction and offer us that second chance as soon as He sees us turn toward Him.

That's good news, indeed. And if you've already been divorced, I encourage you to thank God and embrace that hope. The God of the universe is eager to give you a second chance.

THEY DID IT, AND SO CAN YOU

Just as many ACODs have broken the cycle of divorce started by their parents and grandparents, so it's also true that many who have experienced divorce themselves have taken advantage of a second chance and built strong marriages. You can do the same.

Having gone through divorce by no means
dooms you to permanent marital failure.

I've already mentioned my mom, who got divorced twice before she learned to trust in God and let His love satisfy her soul. She modeled unconditional love, forgiveness, and commitment to my brothers and me. She held us accountable, but always in the context of complete acceptance. She gave us the foundation for believing, despite her own history of broken marriages, that we could succeed in matrimony.

A good friend of mine, married while still in college, came home one day to the news that his wife had fallen in love with his friend and was leaving him for good. Understandably, he was devastated by the divorce that followed.

Later, though, he was given a second chance at marriage. He met a great young woman, and they fell in love and wed. They're now more than 30 years into one of the best marriages I've ever seen, with four great, now-adult children and a growing number of grandchildren to add zest to their middle and later years.

I also mentioned earlier my brother Joe, who—since getting serious with God later in life as our mom did—recovered from his divorce and is now more than 10 years into a strong and vibrant marriage.

Even in the notoriously-unhealthy-for-marriage world of professional entertainers, we can find examples of people who went through divorce but then built lasting unions. Paul Newman, for instance, divorced once before marrying Joanne Woodward, his wife now of almost 50 years at the time of this writing. Actor and later President Ronald Reagan went through a divorce before marrying Nancy, his loving wife of 52 years at the time of his death. And singer Johnny Cash also went through a divorce before marrying June Carter, his beloved wife for 35 years before her death in 2003.

My point is that having gone through divorce, while it makes a second marriage even harder to maintain, by no means dooms you to permanent marital failure. Like many before you, you can succeed.

PRESSING INTO THE FUTURE

There's another scripture that applies well to those of us who need a second chance, whether it's because of divorce or some other regrettable circumstance. It's a statement from the apostle Paul, who wrote, "One thing I do: Forgetting what is behind and straining toward what is ahead, I press on toward the goal."[6] Though Paul wrote in the context of serving God, the principle applies as well to us ACODs who are trying to build lasting marriages.

And the principle is simply this: We need to put past mistakes and past poor choices behind us, and we need to focus on the future.

This doesn't mean, of course, that we completely forget the past. That's not possible. But we don't allow it, no matter how difficult or even painful, to dominate our thinking. We choose instead to focus on the present and the future. We concentrate on those attitudes and those practices that we now know make for success in marriage and in life generally.

So, for example, if we've come to realize that we have a problem with blaming others for our shortcomings, we don't dwell on past instances of that and wallow in guilt. Instead, we ask, "What two-degree change can I make *today* to start overcoming that tendency?" And we can also consider, "If I keep repeating this small change day after day, what kind of progress might I see in a month's time? In six months? In a year?"

As another, more specific example, if we've been prone to starting arguments at the drop of a hat, we might focus on the thought, *Today I'm going to make a point of focusing on the things I appreciate about my spouse and give him or her five sincere compliments. And if I catch myself starting to argue, I will literally bite my tongue (gently) as a reminder to stop immediately and get control of myself.*

We need to learn from the past, but we must not become slaves to it. It's today and tomorrow that we can make positive changes, today and tomorrow that God has given us to do those things that will build a strong marriage.

COMMIT TO THE PERMANENCE OF MARRIAGE

A part of pressing positively into the future is committing ourselves to the permanence of marriage. Our parents didn't model this for us. If we've already been divorced, we have further reason to question whether lifetime marriage really exists.

> *Don't lower your standards. Don't be satisfied with less. Make the commitment and live like you believe it.*

Nonetheless, in our hearts, we know that marriage is meant to last. We know that this is right and that it's what's best for us and our children. So we determine that despite past failures, we believe in the permanence of marriage. It's what we want, and with God's help we're going to strive for that with everything we've got. We won't lower our standards. We won't be satisfied with less.

Then, having made that commitment, we live as if we believe it and mean it. When issues or problems arise in our marriages, we don't look for a way out of the relationship. Instead, we look for ways to work through the issues—preferably, together.

We banish the word *divorce* from our vocabulary in times of disagreement. We refuse to dwell on the notion that we would be better off alone or with someone else. We remind ourselves, *My spouse is my life-mate, not my enemy.* And we take action consistent with our commitment.

A woman once told me candidly, "When my husband does something that really bugs me, it's easy to 'go negative'—to start reciting in my mind all his habits that irritate me. To review all the times that he's ever disappointed or hurt me. Even to start thinking about how much better off I might be without him."

That's dwelling on the past and letting it enslave you.

But this woman continued, "I eventually came to realize that such thinking is useless at best. And at worst, it was really poisoning my attitude toward my husband. So I started praying about it, and God impressed upon me the thought that in such times, I needed to turn my thoughts in an entirely different direction.

"That's when I began to catch myself as quickly as I could in that thought cycle and tell myself, *These thoughts aren't right, and they don't please God.* And then I would start to recite all the things I *admire* about my husband—his hard work, his thoughtfulness (most of the time!), his warm smile, his devotion to me and our children, and so on. And I would ask God to forgive me and to help me forgive and respect my husband."

That's putting the past behind you and taking action consistent with a commitment to your marriage.

GET HELP

Finally, if you've already been divorced, you may need help from others even more than other ACODs. I talked in chapter 6 about the benefits of finding examples to give you hope, to encourage you, and to show you the way to resolve conflict and build healthy relationships. Those benefits apply even more when you've been through marital failure before.

Some good models of unconditional love, acceptance, and successful marriage could make a huge difference in your prospects.

Let's face it. You've had at least one bad experience with the sad and painful end of a marriage. Whatever your exact circumstances, things didn't work out. Statistics say that second marriages fail even more often than first unions. You likely have more concerns and anxieties about your ability to sustain a marriage than someone getting wed for the first time. For all these reasons, some good models of unconditional love, accept-ance, and successful marriage could make a huge difference in your prospects.

Besides examples, you might also want to look for a men-tor—someone older than you, of your same gender, who shares your commitments both to God and to the permanence of marriage, and who has been in a good marriage for a long time. This could be a relative, a friend, a person at your house of worship, or even a counselor. Wherever you find this individ-ual, he or she could be a tremendous asset to you.

When you have questions, your mentor can help you find answers. When you face temptations, your mentor can hold you accountable for making good decisions and taking health-ful actions. When you're discouraged, your mentor can provide the encouragement to hang in there, keep taking the right actions, and trust that things can work out.

Obviously, for such a relationship to work, your mentor needs to be someone you can trust and someone who will have your best interests at heart. You'll need to be honest and candid in describing your thoughts, feelings, and actions, as well as the state of your marriage. And you'll need to be willing to follow your mentor's counsel.

Again, though, if you can find such a person, he or she can be a wonderful help in making your marriage successful.

Remember, too, that the God who gives us second chances

also wants to be actively involved in helping us take advantage of those opportunities. If we're trying to conduct our marriages in a way that honors Him, we can ask for His wisdom and strength in our daily living, like my friend whom I quoted above.

Likewise, we can turn to Scripture for encouragement and wisdom. There we can find assurance of His love and forgiveness. (You might want to read the story of that prodigal young man in Luke 15 every now and then.)

We can also find reminders of His desire to be a consistent, helping presence in our lives. "Never will I leave you," we read; "never will I forsake you."[7]

And there, too, we will find His wisdom for healthy relationships. For example, on the strength to be found in learning from models and mentors, we read, "Two are better than one . . . . If one falls down, his friend can help him up. . . . A cord of three strands is not quickly broken."[8]

The God who observed that "it is not good for the man to be alone," and who declared that "for this reason a man will leave his father and mother and be united to his wife, and they will become one flesh,"[9] wants very much to see your marriage succeed. More than anyone else, He wants to guide, encourage, and empower you to that end.

At any time of day or night, no matter where we are, our heavenly Father is as close as a prayer. Let Him become an active part of your life and your prospects for marital success will increase exponentially.

You Can Succeed

If you've already been divorced, I hope that this entire chapter has been a big dose of encouragement and inspiration for you. Yes, the statistics say that your odds of marital success are slim. But you can beat those odds. With God's help in applying the principles in this chapter and this book, you *can* succeed.

Are you in need of a second chance today? There's a God who's just waiting for you to turn in His direction.

QUESTIONS FOR REFLECTION AND APPLICATION

1. If you've been divorced already, what does it mean to you that God stands ready to give you a second chance?

2. What past mistakes do you need to put behind you in order to press ahead into a positive future?

3. If you need additional help in overcoming the effects of a divorce, where might that help come from? If an answer doesn't come readily to mind, where could you start looking?

FROM A CURSE
TO A BLESSING

*The great truth that can more than conquer the
curse is that through your power of choice and
God's power to help you carry out what you know
to be right thoughts, words, and actions, you can
begin today to move in a positive direction.*

At the beginning of this book, I wrote that the biblical picture of being "under a curse" is that of a stream that has been dammed up. Consequently, no life-giving water is flowing. And that's a vivid picture of the curse under which we've grown up—you and I—when we've grown up in homes of divorce.

As we've seen in the pages of this book, however, we don't have to stay under that curse. Or, to return to our imagery, by following the principles we've explored here, we can poke holes in that dam and see it gradually break down completely, releasing the flow of clean, fresh water we so desperately need.

In the desert, we can see lush and fragrant and riotously colorful flowers bloom.

Let me tell you the story of a woman we'll call Kelly. Talk about growing up under a curse! If there has ever been anyone the odds were stacked up against for building and sustaining a strong and healthy marriage, it was Kelly. Kelly's situation makes her the perfect poster child for just how difficult some children of divorce can have it.

Kelly grew up in a family in which her grandparents were divorced. Then Kelly's own parents divorced.

Not only that, but both her mom and her dad were from families of six children, and in both cases, three of the six siblings divorced. One of Kelly's uncles, by himself, kept a law firm's worth of attorneys busy—he was married *eight* times!

Kelly herself was one of eight children in her parents' family. All those children are grown now, and all got married. But only three are still married to their original spouses. Some have been married numerous times.

Over the years, as you might imagine, a number of children were born to Kelly's siblings. Many of those nieces and nephews are now grown, too—and many of them are already divorced as well.

You can see, then, why I call Kelly an icon for "child of divorce." Clearly, unfortunately, marriage as a lifetime commitment, "till death do us part," is not the norm in her family. It's not what she saw modeled. No one could blame her for wondering if such a relationship is truly possible.

And yet . . .

Despite growing up in such circumstances, at the time of

this writing, Kelly and her husband have been married for 31 years and counting.

Has their relationship had its lows as well as its highs? Sure. Is it hassle-free and conflict-free? Of course not. But do they love each other deeply? And are they committed to each other and to the relationship, to working out their "issues" and facing life and its challenges *together*? Absolutely.

> *I call Kelly an icon for "child of divorce."*
> *And yet as of this writing, she and*
> *her husband have been married*
> *for 31 years and counting.*

They are, if you will, a magnificent red rosebush in a mostly barren landscape.

How did this happen?

Growing . . . Together

Kelly and her husband have built and sustained a strong marriage the same way you can, using the principles and strategies discussed in this book.

Through commitment to each other and to the relationship, they have grown closer together over the years rather than letting Kelly's curse of being an ACOD tear them apart.

Like you, they have the power to choose how they will respond to whatever life throws at them. They choose, day by day, to love, to resolve differences, to forgive and reconcile when necessary, and to put the needs of the other above their own when *that's* needed.

Kelly has been known to joke, "If I weren't so stubborn, determined to make my own marriage work, we might have been divorced several times by now!"

As you need to do, Kelly has faced her fears and "stepped out of the trailer" to deal with her issues growing out of being an ACOD—to move toward health. She'll tell you that she still struggles with the manifestations of the curse. It's not easy, and even having a good spouse doesn't make those problems just go away. Again, it's a daily—sometimes moment-by-moment—choice.

When all they can manage, even with His help, is a step or two "out of the trailer" and in the right direction, they trust that God is going to show up, honor their good intentions, and do for them those things that only He can do.

Furthermore, Kelly and her husband have found models to learn from, examples of unconditional love, of healthy marital relationship, and of commitment. They've seen successful marriages in action. They know it can be done, despite the negative track record in Kelly's family.

Most especially, Kelly and her spouse have crafted a marriage of more than 31 years by drawing on the love and power of God. When they need wisdom beyond their own to solve a problem or overcome some obstacle, they seek it first in prayer.

When they know the life-giving thing to say or do but they just can't summon the strength from within to follow through, they ask God for His power.

And when all they can manage, even with His help, is a step or two "out of the trailer" and in the right direction, they trust that God is going to show up, honor their good intentions, and do for them those things that only He can do.

The sad truth is that being an adult child of divorce has put you under a curse. But the great truth that can more than conquer the curse is that through your power of choice and God's power to help you carry out what you know to be right thoughts, words, and actions, you can begin today to move in a positive direction.

Today, you can start to reverse the curse.

Today, you can take those first steps, initiate that first two-degree change, to overcome the manifestations of the curse in your life.

Today, you can begin to break the cycle of divorce in which you and your family have been trapped. In so doing, you will not only make a far better life for yourself, but you will also bless future generations—your own children and grandchildren, and many generations yet to come.

The choice is yours.

Notes

Introduction

1. Judith S. Wallerstein, Julia M. Lewis, and Sandra Blakeslee, *The Unexpected Legacy of Divorce* (New York: Hyperion, 2000), p. xiii.
2. Beverly and Tom Rodgers, "Pain and Triumph for Children of Divorce," on www.soulhealinglove.com, 1/13/05, citing The Heritage Foundation's report "The Effects of Divorce on America," 6/5/00.
3. "Children of Divorce Getting Divorced Themselves; Becoming Teen Moms, Single Moms, Battered Wives," on http://divorcereform.org/teenmoms.html, 7/15/04.

Chapter 1

1. Toby Green, "Custody and Safekeeping," Body & Soul, 11/18/01, on www.tobygreen.com, 1/13/05.
2. Beverly and Tom Rodgers, "Pain and Triumph for Children of Divorce," on www.soulhealinglove.com, 1/13/05, citing The Heritage Foundation's report "The Effects of Divorce on America," 6/5/00.
3. "Divorce Statistics" on www.co.midland.mi.us, 1/14/05.
4. Leslie Carbone, "The Divorce Caste," on www.pfm.org, 1/14/05.

5. Cara Williams in "Survey suggests parental breakup may affect child's marriage prospects in adulthood," Canadian Press, 9/11/01, on www.fact.on.ca, 1/14/05.

6. Gary A. Sprague, "Breaking the Cycle," *Single-Parent Family*, Focus on the Family, 01/96.

Chapter 2

1. Peg Tyre, "Trend Toward Solitary Confinement Worries Experts," www.cnn.com/US/9801/09/solitary .confinement/#1.

2. Ecclesiastes 4:9-10

Chapter 3

1. 1 Corinthians 15:33

2. Cohabitors 46% more likely to divorce (Andrew Herrmann, "20-somethings who have witnessed ugly divorces in no rush to repeat error," *Chicago Sun-Times*, 6/10/03, on www.suntimes.com/special-sections/ marriage, 1/13/05).

3. Proverbs 13:12

Chapter 4

1. 1 John 2:11

Chapter 5

1. Everett L. Worthington, Jr., and R. Kirby Worthington, "No Excuses," www.christianitytoday.com, 1/13/05.
2. 2 Kings 21:5-6
3. 2 Kings 21:20-21
4. 2 Kings 22:2
5. Karen L. Maudlin, "Children of Divorce," www.christianitytoday.com, 1/14/05.
6. See *The Two-Degree Difference* and *Heart Shift* (Broadman & Holman).
7. Proverbs 11:14, NASB.
8. Matthew 10:29-31
9. 1 Peter 5:7
10. Ephesians 2:4
11. 1 John 4:16
12. Psalm 69:16
13. Psalm 86:5
14. Psalm 100:5
15. John 3:16
16. Deuteronomy 23:4-5 (emphasis added)
17. Philippians 2:13
18. Philippians 4:13

Chapter 6

1. Pamela Paul, *The Starter Marriage and the Future of Matrimony* (New York: Random House, 2002) as

quoted in Karen S. Peterson, "Starter Marriage: A new term for early divorce," *USA Today*, 1/29/02, p. 8D.

Chapter 7
1. Deuteronomy 30:19

Chapter 8
1. Elizabeth Marquardt, *Between Two Worlds* (New York: Crown, 2005), p. 189.
2. Ibid., p. 191.

Chapter 9
1. Luke 15:12
2. Luke 15:13
3. Ibid.
4. Luke 15:22-23
5. Luke 15:24
6. Philippians 3:13-14
7. Hebrews 13:5
8. Ecclesiastes 4:9, 10, 12
9. Genesis 2:18, 24

Recommended Resources

General

Ron L. Deal, *The Smart Stepfamily* (Minneapolis: Bethany House, 2006)

Elizabeth Marquardt, *Between Two Worlds* (New York: Crown, 2005)

John Trent, *Choosing to Live the Blessing* (Colorado Springs, Colo.: WaterBrook, 1997)

Judith S. Wallerstein, Julia M. Lewis, and Sandra Blakeslee, *The Unexpected Legacy of Divorce* (New York: Hyperion, 2000)

Feeling isolated

Randy Carlson, *Starved for Affection* (Carol Stream, Ill.: Tyndale/Focus on the Family, 2005)

Sharon Hersh, *Bravehearts: Unlocking the Courage to Love with Abandon* (Colorado Springs, Colo.: WaterBrook, 2000)—for women

False guilt

Henry Cloud, *Changes That Heal: How to Understand Your Past to Ensure a Healthier Future* (Grand Rapids, Mich.: Zondervan, 1997)

James C. Dobson, *Emotions: Can You Trust Them?* (Ventura, Calif.: Regal, 2003)

Unhealthy family secrets

Dave Carder, Earl Henslin, John Townsend, Henry Cloud, and Alice Brawand, *Secrets of Your Family Tree: Healing for Adult Children of Dysfunctional Families* (Chicago: Moody, 1995)

Henry Cloud, *Changes That Heal: How to Understand Your Past to Ensure a Healthier Future* (Grand Rapids, Mich.: Zondervan, 1997)

Marsha Means, *Living with Your Husband's Secret Wars* (Grand Rapids, Mich.: Revell, 1999)

Patrick Means, *Men's Secret Wars* (Grand Rapids, Mich.: Revell, 1999)

Fear-based procrastination

Carol Kent, *Tame Your Fears and Transform Them into Faith, Confidence, and Action* (Colorado Springs, Colo.: Nav-Press, 2003)—for women

John C. Maxwell, *Failing Forward: Turning Mistakes into Stepping Stones for Success* (Nashville: Nelson, 2000)

Making poor choices

Dave Carder, Earl Henslin, John Townsend, Henry Cloud, and Alice Brawand, *Secrets of Your Family Tree: Healing for*

Adult Children of Dysfunctional Families (Chicago: Moody, 1995)

Henry Cloud, *Changes That Heal: How to Understand Your Past to Ensure a Healthier Future* (Grand Rapids, Mich.: Zondervan, 1997)

Henry Cloud and John Townsend, *Boundaries in Marriage* (Grand Rapids, Mich.: Zondervan, 2002)

James C. Dobson, *Emotions: Can You Trust Them?* (Ventura, Calif.: Regal, 2003)

A habit of making false starts

Gary and Barbara Rosberg, *Divorce-Proof Your Marriage* (Carol Stream, Ill.: Tyndale, 2003)

Breaking commitments

Alistair Begg, *Lasting Love: How to Avoid Marital Failure* (Chicago: Moody, 2002)

Al Janssen, *The Marriage Masterpiece* (Carol Stream, Ill.: Tyndale/Focus on the Family, 2001)

Les and Leslie Parrott, *When Bad Things Happen to Good Marriages: How to Stay Together When Life Pulls You Apart* (Grand Rapids, Mich.: Zondervan, 2001)—referring to marital commitments

Jim Talley, *Reconcilable Differences* (Nashville: Nelson, 1991)—referring to marital commitments

Blaming others

Alistair Begg, *Lasting Love: How to Avoid Marital Failure* (Chicago: Moody, 2002)

Henry Cloud and John Townsend, *Boundaries in Marriage* (Grand Rapids, Mich.: Zondervan, 2002)

Gary Smalley, *The DNA of Relationships: How You Are Designed for Satisfying Relationships* (Carol Stream, Ill.: Tyndale, 2004)

Smoldering anger/inability to forgive

Archibald Hart, "Resentment: The Cancer of Emotions," Focus on the Family broadcast CD

R. T. Kendall, *Total Forgiveness* (Lake Mary, Fla.: Charisma, 2002)

Grace Ketterman and David Hazard, *When You Can't Say "I Forgive You": Breaking the Bonds of Anger and Hurt* (Colorado Springs, Colo.: NavPress, 2000)

Gary Rosberg, *Healing the Hurt in Your Marriage* (Carol Stream, Ill.: Tyndale/Focus on the Family, 2004)

Gary Smalley, "Overcoming Anger," Focus on the Family broadcast cassette

Neil Clark Warren, *Make Anger Your Ally* (Carol Stream, Ill.: Tyndale/Focus on the Family, 1990)

Not really listening to others

Gary Chapman, *Covenant Marriage: Building Communication & Intimacy* (Nashville: Broadman & Holman, 2003)

James C. Dobson, *Five Essentials for Lifelong Intimacy* (Sisters, Ore.: Multnomah, 2005)

Archibald D. Hart and Sharon Hart Morris, *Safe Haven Marriage: Building a Relationship You Want to Come Home To* (Nashville: W Publishing Group, 2003)

Les and Leslie Parrott, *Love Talk: Speak Each Other's Language Like You Never Have Before* (Grand Rapids, Mich.: Zondervan, 2004)

Gary Rosberg, *Healing the Hurt in Your Marriage* (Carol Stream, Ill.: Tyndale/Focus on the Family, 2004)

Seeing God only as an impersonal, uncaring being

Steve and Dee Brestin, *Building Your House on the Lord: A Firm Foundation for Family Life* (Colorado Springs, Colo.: Shaw, 2003)

Les Carter and Frank Minirth, *The Freedom from Depression Workbook* (Nashville: Nelson, 1995)

Max Lucado, *He Still Moves Stones* (Nashville: W Publishing Group, 1999)

Lysa Terkeurst, *Who Holds the Key to Your Heart?* (Chicago: Moody/Focus on the Family, 2002)—for women

Gary Thomas, *Sacred Marriage* (Grand Rapids, Mich.: Zondervan, 2002)

The value of mentors/accountability when trying to make positive choices

Henry Cloud, *Changes That Heal: How to Understand Your Past to Ensure a Healthier Future* (Grand Rapids, Mich.: Zondervan, 1997)

How to have a successful marriage when you've already been divorced

Joseph Warren Kniskern, *Making a New Vow: A Christian's Guide to Remarrying After Divorce* (Nashville: Broadman & Holman, 2003)

Kevin Leman, *Becoming a Couple of Promise* (Colorado Springs, Colo.: NavPress, 1999)

Gary Smalley, *FOF Marriage Series: The Blended Marriage* (Ventura, Calif.: Gospel Light, 2004)

How to overcome your fears when trying to make positive changes

Henry Cloud, *Changes That Heal: How to Understand Your Past to Ensure a Healthier Future* (Grand Rapids, Mich.: Zondervan, 1997)

Carol Kent, *Tame Your Fears and Transform Them into Faith, Confidence, and Action* (Colorado Springs, Colo.: NavPress, 2003)—for women

The wisdom in making a series of small, positive changes rather than trying to make huge changes all at once
John Trent, *Heart Shift* (Nashville: Broadman & Holman, 2004)

John Trent, *The Two-Degree Difference* (Nashville: Broadman & Holman, 2006)

DR. JOHN TRENT is president and founder of the Center for StrongFamilies in Scottsdale, Arizona, where he trains lay leaders and pastors to launch family ministry programs at their home churches. In addition to his work at the Center, Dr. Trent is a best-selling author and sought-after speaker at retreats, conferences, churches, and seminars across the country.

In addition to his StrongFamilies in Stressful Times Seminar, Dr. Trent also speaks regularly to corporate America on work/life balance and Leading from Your Strengths. He has been a featured speaker at the YPO Global Leadership Conference, numerous Young Presidents' Organization chapter events, and Family Universities. In addition, he's spoken to numerous individual companies such as Chick-fil-A, Northwestern Insurance, The Walt Disney Corporation, Universal Studios, The United States Army, The United States Coast Guard Academy, and many others.

John has been a featured guest on television and radio programs such as the *Oprah Winfrey Show, Focus on the Family, Insight for Living,* the *Billy Graham Evangelistic Association, The 700 Club, Chapel of the Air, Talk to the Doctors, Life Perspectives,* Moody Broadcasting's *Prime Time, Parent Talk, Family Radio,* and many more.

Dr. Trent is the author or co-author of more than a dozen best-selling, award-winning books, including his latest, *The Two-Degree Difference.*

Visit the Web site at http://www.StrongFamilies.com.

LARRY WEEDEN serves as director of book development for Focus on the Family. A veteran of more than 25 years in Christian publishing, he has worked with authors including Chuck Colson, John Maxwell, Gary Smalley, Patsy Clairmont, and many others. He's also an active freelance writer, with more than 16 books to his credit, including *Feeling Guilty, Finding Grace* and the recently released *Wired by God* (co-authored with Joe White).

FOCUS ON THE FAMILY®

Welcome to the family!

Whether you purchased this book, borrowed it, or received it as a gift, we're glad you're reading it. It's just one of the many helpful, encouraging, and biblically based resources produced by Focus on the Family for people in all stages of life.

Focus began in 1977 with the vision of one man, Dr. James Dobson, a licensed psychologist and author of numerous best-selling books on marriage, parenting, and family. Alarmed by the societal, political, and economic pressures that were threatening the existence of the American family, Dr. Dobson founded Focus on the Family with one employee and a once-a-week radio broadcast aired on 36 stations.

Now an international organization reaching millions of people daily, Focus on the Family is dedicated to preserving values and strengthening and encouraging families through the life-changing message of Jesus Christ.

Focus on the Family Magazines

These faith-building, character-developing publications address the interests, issues, concerns, and challenges faced by every member of your family from preschool through the senior years.

| Focus on the Family **Citizen®** U.S. news issues | Focus on the Family **Clubhouse Jr.™** Ages 4 to 8 | Focus on the Family **Clubhouse™** Ages 8 to 12 | **Breakaway®** Teen guys | **Brio®** Teen girls 12 to 16 | **Brio & Beyond®** Teen girls 16 to 19 | **Plugged In®** Reviews movies, music, TV |

More Great Resources
from Focus on the Family®

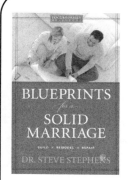

BLUEPRINTS FOR A SOLID MARRIAGE
Whether your marriage "house" needs it's simplysomea minor repairs, remodeling, or major reconstruction, *Blueprints for a Solid Marriage* helps time-strapped couples quickly assess and enhance their relationship to determine what is needed.s Dr. Steve Stephens gives couples by laying the foundation and tools for marital bliss to improve any marriage with through engaging stories, and along witha fun and easy to understand detailed plan for "marriage improvement projects." (Hardcover)

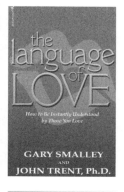

THE LANGUAGE OF LOVE
The frustration of missing out on meaningful communication affects not only our marriages, but also our friendships, parent-child and professional relationships. Gary Smalley and John Trent deliver a time-tested method that enables us to bridge communication gaps, opening the door to greater intimacy and delivering lasting change! (Paperback with study guide)

THE TWO SIDES OF LOVE
Best-selling authors and family experts Gary Smalley and John Trent explain how to find a healthy balance between the protective, consistent "hardside" love and the tender, understanding "softside" love. By examining the four basic personality types, you'll learn how to best demonstrate both sides of love in all your relationships—and experience wholehearted love! (Paperback with study guide)

FOR MORE INFORMATION

Online:
Log on to www.family.org
In Canada, log on to www.focusonthefamily.ca.

Phone:
Call toll free: (800) A-FAMILY
In Canada, call toll free: (800) 661-9800.